# THE BEER LOVER'S GUIDE TO
# CRICKET

# THE BEER LOVER'S GUIDE TO
# CRICKET

## ROGER PROTZ

CAMRA
BOOKS

*Dedicated to the memory
of Fred Trueman (1931-2006)
who took 307 Test wickets
in 67 matches and enjoyed a jar*

Published by Campaign for Real Ale
230 Hatfield Road, St Albans
Hertfordshire AL1 4LW

www.camra.org.uk/books

© Campaign for Real Ale 2007

ISBN: 978-1-85249-227-4

A CIP catalogue record for this book is available
from the British Library

Printed in Singapore by KHL Printing Co Pte Ltd

Head of Publications: Joanna Copestick
Publications Project Editor: Debbie Williams
Editorial Assistance: Emma Lloyd
Design: Karen Bowen
Picture Research: Sarah Airey and Nadine Bazar
Marketing Manager: Georgina Rudman

## Key to symbols

- **Real Fire:** a fire fuelled by coal, smokeless fuel or logs
- **Q** Quiet pub: free from piped music, jukeboxes, electronic games and TVs (at least one room)
- **Family room:** where the licensee guarantees that families are warmly (and legally) welcome in their own separate room, not a corridor or a corner of the main bar or lounge
- **Outdoor drinking area:** this may vary from a garden to benches on a pave ment, or even a village green
- **Accommodation:** rooms to let (no assessment of quality or price is made)
- **Lunchtime meals:** not snacks but substantial fare (including one hot dish) and in the pub itself, not in a separate restaurant
- **Evening meals:** as for lunchtime meals; separate restaurants are often mentioned in the pub description
- **Public bar:** a traditional public bar, where the beer may be cheaper
- **Wheelchair access:** easy access to the pub and WCs
- **Camping:** camping facilities for tents at the pub or within one mile; sometimes caravans are also welcomed and this is often mentioned
- **Near railway station:** within half a mile, sometimes including steam or electric railways, which are then often mentioned: the name of the nearest station is only given if it differs from the name of the town or village itselft Bus routes that regularly pass close to pubs
- **Near underground, metro or tram station:** within half a mile: station names are only given if different to those of the town, village or city area
- **Traditional pub games played**
- **Real draught cider** (not keg cider) available
- **P** Pub has its own car park
- **Smoking area provided outside:** if covered or heated this is often mentioned
- **Oversized lined pint glasses:** used for some or all beers

# CONTENTS

# PUTTING THE BAILS ON

The inspiration for this book was a visit in 2005 to the Bat and Ball in Hambledon to see how the venerable old inn had recovered from the trauma of being turned, briefly and unsuccessfully, into a restaurant, with all the historic cricketing memorabilia chucked out. I found the pub safe in the hands of George Gale & Co, a family-owned brewery in nearby Horndean, and marvelled at the collection of old photographs, ancient bats and balls and other memorabilia that had been restored to the pub. The result was a short article in the 2006 edition of the Good Beer Guide and the growing realisation that the powerful link between cricket, pubs and beer might be worthy of greater attention.

There is no shortage of books about cricket. It is one of the most written-about sports on the planet. But I wanted to emphasise the link between the game and the enjoyment of good beer. Players and spectators at Hambledon quaffed Richard Nyren's ale from the Bat and Ball before, during and after matches. The tradition continues. It was clear from the triumphal tour of London in 2005 on an open-top bus by the England cricket team, victors of that unforgettable Ashes series, that liquid refreshment had been taken on board. Beer and cricket exist at a less vaulted level. Until the licensing laws changed in England, the pattern of Sunday club cricket was tried and tested: meet in the pub at 1pm, enjoy a beer, talk tactics, discuss the batting and bowling orders, then repair to the ground in time for a 2pm start. At 6pm the umpires would call 'Twenty overs', and by 7pm the game would end and the pub would be open again.

Modern cricket developed at Hambledon, with not only tactics but also the actual laws of the game discussed and codified in the Bat and Ball. Other pubs had a part to play. The club that became MCC was hatched in the Star and Garter in London's Pall Mall and played, with the help of Thomas Lord, at White Conduit Fields alongside a pub in Islington. Many publicans rented their grounds to cricket clubs as the game grew in popularity. As power shifted in England from the landed gentry to the new industrialists, breweries supplied players and sponsorship.

It became clear, as I researched the first-class grounds, that there is a wealth of historic material available for cricket lovers to see and enjoy. I knew, of course, that Lord's had a museum but discovered that many other grounds also had museums or displays worthy of attention. I am fascinated by the history of cricket, much of which is enshrined in the museums, with their images of the game that take it from whiskery gents in top hats to modern players in helmets and breastplates. I was also anxious to rescue Hambledon from an evocative but false picture of a

village in the eighteenth century that was a late extension of 'Merrie England', with duke and dairyman happily cricketing on the green. It was nothing like that. It was a time of deep social division and, after the Napoleonic Wars, also one of desperate rural poverty. But at the same time, in a brief period of history, the duke and the dairyman did combine to transform a game from a rural pastime into the one we recognise today.

To celebrate the noble game, I have visited all the First-Class County grounds and detail here the memorabilia that is on display in many of them, memorabilia that helps deepen our knowledge and appreciation of the history and development of the game. Along the way, I have visited some fine pubs close to each ground where readers can enjoy excellent cask beer. In a few cases, good beer is also available at the grounds and I hope other counties can be encouraged to follow suit.

The book, in short, is a celebration of both a game and a style of beer that are rich in tradition and part of the warp and weft of British society. Drink deep and enjoy, and remember – even when rain stops play – there is a good pub close at hand.

# HAMBLEDON,
## *where the ale flared like turpentine*

*A sketch of the Bat & Ball at Hambledon in 1978 (left) shows how little it had changed since the eighteenth century. The pub today (previous page) is still commemorated as the birthplace of the modern game of cricket.*

' *There was high feasting held on Broadhalfpenny during the solemnity of one of our grand matches. Oh! It was a heart-stirring sight to witness the multitude forming a complete and dense circle round that noble green. Half the county would be present, and all their hearts with us – Little Hambledon, pitted against all England was a proud thought for the Hampshire men. Defeat was glory in such a struggle – victory, indeed, made us only "a little lower than angels". How those fine brawn-faced fellows of farmers would drink to our success! And then, what stuff they had to drink! – Punch! – not your new Punch à la Romaine, or Ponche à la Groseille, or your modern cat-lap milk punch – punch be-devilled; but good, unsophisticated John Bull stuff, – stark! – that would stand on end – punch that would make a cat speak! Sixpence a bottle! We had not sixty millions of interest to pay in those days. The ale, too! – not the modern horror under the same name that drives as many men melancholy-mad as the hypocrites do; – not the beastliness of these days, that will make a fellow's inside like a shaking bog – and as rotten; but barley-corn, such as would put the souls of three butchers into one weaver. Ale that would flare like turpentine – genuine Boniface! – This immortal viand (for it was more than liquor) was vended at twopence per pint.* ' JOHN NYREN

The bibulous memories quoted above are those of John Nyren, son of Richard Nyren, who was the landlord of the Bat and Ball pub in Hambledon in the late eighteenth century and also the driving force behind the cricket team that played on Broadhalfpenny Down across the road. John was born in 1764 and he grew to manhood at the same time as Hambledon achieved fame as the greatest cricket club in England. John's reminiscences appeared in a London magazine, The Town, in 1832 and were reproduced in book form a year later. He was recalling more than just the drinking habits in his father's pub. In a brief period of time, the game of cricket evolved on Broadhalfpenny (pronounced 'Broadhappeny') Down from a simple, rustic one with curved bats like hockey sticks, a tiny wicket with two stumps, and underarm bowling in to the game we recognise today.

The origins of cricket are obscure, medieval and may even be – perish the thought – French. Unlike sports rooted in the towns, football in particular, cricket and other games played with sticks (cricks) and balls were firmly bucolic, played by shepherds and other country folk. Rural games such as stool-ball, stow-ball, tip-cat and cat-in-the-hole have long since disappeared, though stool-ball mutated into rounders and was exported to the United

States where it mutated again into baseball. Cricket, criquet or creag is recorded from as early as 1300 when the Royal Wardrobe paid £6 to enable Prince Edward, aged 15, later Edward II, to play at creag. The prince had a friend, Piers Gaveston, who came from Gascony, a fact that stimulated the belief that the game may have arrived from across the Channel at the time of the invasion of 1066. The Norman aristocracy would not have indulged in a rough, plebeian game that required a ball to be bashed by a stick, preferring the more chivalric [sic] pursuits of hunting or the tournament, but the lower orders were free to indulge. Nevertheless, cricket and its derivatives remained minor sports for several centuries. Successive governments that cracked down on rowdy games that encouraged violence or excessive gambling included football and even bowls, but cricket is rarely if ever mentioned. It reappears in 1598 in Guildford, Surrey, when John Derrick testified in a lawsuit over disputed common land that he had played cricket there as a schoolboy. By the early sixteenth century, as the Puritan backlash against all things un-Godly was gathering pace, there are several instances of men being fined for playing cricket instead of attending to their devotions. In 1629, Henry Cuffen, the curate of Ruckinge on Romney Marsh, was censured for 'playing at Cricketts' immediately after evening prayers. A Puritan minister, Thomas Wilson, complained that Maidstone was 'a very prophane town where Morrice-dancing, Cudgels, Stoolball, Crickets' were played 'openly and publicly on the Lord's Day'. In nearby Cox Heath in 1646 a game of cricket was played on open land for a wager of 12 candles. More serious betting was to flood the game in succeeding centuries.

Cromwell's Protectorate outlawed bear-baiting, bull-baiting, cock-fighting, gambling and any activities that attracted crowds that might threaten public order. Cricket, save for when it encouraged people to miss church services, escaped stricture. It began to blossom during the Restoration due mainly to changing fashions in the countryside. Cromwell's revolution had been an incomplete one. Unlike the French Revolution, when the aristocracy was despatched by the guillotine, the English upper class remained largely intact. It had kept a collective low profile during the Protectorate but hung on to its vast estates.

But now the balance of forces changed. Parliamentarians, yeoman and gentry who had been awarded large parcels of land seized from the crown and the church, began to challenge the power of the aristocracy. Men who had been the backbone and breastplate of the New Model Army were also firm believers in the New Model Economy. They had no truck with the old feudal ways of country life. They thought agriculture should be a business and to that end they set about enclosing land, turning strip farmers into wage labourers and introducing modern machinery to reap and sow. There are many complex reasons why Hambledon's role as the chief cricket club in England was a brief one but, as we shall see, one was the impoverishment of the countryside and its people, and the inexorable drift to London and other burgeoning towns and cities.

But at first the old nobility held sway and revelled in the return of the monarchy, even though the king was now nominally controlled by parliament. The old 'sports' of cock-fighting and bear-baiting returned, but they were no longer as popular and went into decline. The nobility were inveterate gamblers and looked for new sports to indulge their passion. Horse racing blossomed, Broadhalfpenny Down for a time staged horse races as well as cricket matches, and cricket quickly attracted the attentions of the rich. It was a game of such wild fluctuations of fortune, with teams often snatching defeat from the jaws of victory, that it offered tempting bait to gamblers.

Cricket spread rapidly in the eighteenth century in southern and central England. With a rising demand for grain and meat from the cities, wages and other forms of incomes grew and the working population in the country-side had more leisure time to either play sport or watch it. Villages developed teams that played on a regular basis and records show that publicans were quick to see a new line of business. They built beer tents on cricket grounds to offer refreshment to spectators and, if no suitable pitch was available, offered their own pub land in order that matches could be played. Two grounds that were to become important venues for cricket in London, the Artillery Ground and White Conduit House, were attached to pubs, while the Marylebone Cricket Club grew out of meetings held at the Star and Garter tavern in Pall Mall, a street named after a long extinct game that involved hitting a ball with a

*Previous page, The main bar of the pub, with many old cricket photos and an ancient curved bat. It was the deadly bowling of 'Lumpy' Stevens (right) that led to the addition of the third stump, part of the transformation of the game in the eighteenth century. Below, some of the books and memorabilia on display in the pub.*

*Francis Hayman's celebrated painting The Game of Cricket as Played in the Artillery Ground, London, 1743, gives a fascinating image of the game before the Hambledon revolution. The wicket is tiny and has just two stumps, bowling is underarm and the bat is curved like a hockey stick. In common with many grounds in the eighteenth century, the Artillery was attached to a public house.*

stick through a hoop. It was here that the first rules or laws of cricket were drawn up.

If cricket was played widely in Hampshire, Kent, Surrey and Sussex in the eighteenth century, why was it that one village, its pub and its cricket ground rose to prominence? Why did Hambledon, a remote place even today, reached by narrow roads, attract crowds of 20,000 to watch matches, some played against 'All England'? And how did just one club become, before the arrival of MCC, the arbiter of the laws of the game? There are several reasons. The area had a preponderance of powerful landowners, including John Sackville, who was the third Duke of Dorset, Lord Tankerville and Sir Horace Mann who, as a result of their prodigious wealth and power, could afford to pay talented cricketers to play the

game. Mann, for example, took on one Hambledon player, James Aylward, as his bailiff. Aylward was a disaster at the job but he remained in Mann's employ as Sir Horace, whose obituary reported him as 'rather dedicated to pleasure than business', needed good players and a strong team to enable him to bet successfully on matches. John Nyren claimed that all Hambledon matches were played for stakes of £500 a side, enormous sums for the time.

Hambledon and its environs were fortunate in having more than its fair share of good cricketers. Such players as the farmer Thomas Brett, Edward 'Lumpy' Stevens, who was a retainer of Lord Tankerville's, the carpenter Tom Sueter, George Leer, who was a brewer, Peter 'Buck' Stewart, William Hogsflesh, John Small, a shoemaker,

an important distinction at the time. He was not only a good innkeeper but was also an excellent cricketer, a 'cunning' left-arm bowler and hard-hitting batsmen who had picked up the skills from his celebrated cricketing uncle, Richard Newland of Slindon in Sussex. It was Nyren's passion for the game that built the club's reputation and kept it together in good times as well as bad.

The choice of Broadhalfpenny Down is an odd one, despite the proximity of the pub. It is a good mile outside the village and a white line on the floor of the Bat and Ball marks the boundary between Hambledon and the neighbouring village of Clanfield. The ground is high, with fine views of the surrounding countryside, the sea and the distant chalk cliffs of the Isle of Wight. But it can be bleak when the sun goes in and wind and rain obscure the view. It was probably the down's role as common land for sheep grazing and later as a horse racing track that encouraged cricket to be played there as well: before the invention of the mower, sheep were used to crop cricket pitches. But Broadhalfpenny never entirely suited the nobility, who often bought their ladies to watch the game from closed carriages, and Lord Dorset later moved the club to the less exposed Windmill Down closer to the village.

In spite of its later celebrity, the origins of the Hambledon club are vague, due to the loss of vital records in a fire that destroyed the pavilion at Lord's. It is believed that the club was formed in the 1750s. The earliest record is of a game played in 1756 when the Reading Mercury reported that a dog had been lost during a cricket match on Broadhalfpenny Down in August of that year. Also in 1756, Hambledon played Dartford, one of the strongest teams in southern England, on the Artillery Ground in London. Then Hambledon disappeared for several years. The founder of the club, Squire Thomas Land, died in 1767 and responsibility for the club was taken up a local clergyman, the Rev Charles Powlett or Paulett. He was rather different to the modern clergyman, being the illegitimate son of the thoroughly dissolute Duke of Bolton and his mistress and later wife, Lavinia Fenton, who played Polly Peachum in the first production of John Gay's The Beggar's Opera. Charles's activities and bad company in London forced his family to send him to the obscurity of a Hampshire parish. But old habits die hard, and it seems

and William Barber, a publican, left their mark on the early game and influenced its future course. As the club's reputation grew, it was able to attract other fine players from further afield: Noah Mann from Petworth, the Walker brothers from Surrey, John Wells and the Beldham brothers, George and William, all from Farnham, and the potter David Harris from Odiham, a fearsome, fast underarm bowler. This was a cricket team *sui generis*.

In to this fascinating social mix of nobles and commoners came the combustible force of Richard Nyren. He turned his pub, first called simply the Hut, into the Bat and Ball where all social classes could converse and carouse. His nicknames of 'The Guv'nor' and 'the General' sum up his power and prestige: he also owned a farm and considered himself a yeoman rather than a publican, his main interest in the local cricket club was the ability it offered him to continue his gambling. It took the steady yeoman hand of Richard Nyren to run the playing side, which he also captained.

At first Hambledon was extravagantly successful. In 1767 the club won two matches by the substantial margins of 262 and 224 'notches'. In the days before delineated boundaries, there were no 'fours' and 'sixes': batsmen had to score by running (two Hambledon players once ran ten) and scorers cut notches in sticks to mark the runs. The following year, Hambledon took on the might of Kent and defeated the county. But success was followed by a slump in form, so bad that by 1771 there was considerable doubt that the club could continue. In that year Hambledon suffered a humiliating 10-wickets defeat against All England at Guildford. Vast sums, running into many thousands of pounds, were wagered on the match and it seems the crisis at Hambledon was caused not so much by the lack of success but the losses sustained by wealthy backers.

A crisis meeting was called late in the season at the Bat and Ball and some members argued that the club should be wound up. But Powlett, Nyren and their supporters passionately declared the club should continue and the meeting agreed a stay of execution until one last match was played that year. Fatefully, it was against Surrey at Chertsey on 23 September. The purse for the match was for the relatively small sum of £50 but Hambledon's future rested on the outcome. It went down in history as a celebrated game as Hambledon scrambled home to victory by a single notch and then went on to lay down a new law of the game as a result of the activities of one Surrey player, Thomas 'Shock' White. He strode out to bat carrying a blade that was six inches across, almost as wide as the wicket. In spite of this mighty bludgeon, he failed to make many notches but, on their return to Hambledon, a meeting between the club captain and two of his principal players decreed that 'In view of the performance of Mr White of Ryegate [sic] on September 23rd that four and quarter inches shall be the breadth [of a bat] forthwith. This day 25th day of September 1771. Richard Nyren, T. Brett, J. Small.' In spite of the club's loss of form that season, Hambledon had sufficient clout to

have that ruling incorporated into the official laws of the game. Nyren ordered for the club an iron frame that would accept a bat of the required, legal width if there were any doubts about its correct size. The frame was kept in the Bat and Ball for several years.

So Hambledon continued. Membership of the club was expensive, three guineas a year, more than a month's pay for a labourer. Most of the members were titled nobility, army and navy officers, clergymen, MPs or wine merchants. The players were paid on a match-by-match basis at the rate of four shillings for a win and three shillings for a loss, with additional money for hire of horses for travel to games and overnight accommodation. It boosted the income of labourers but not sufficient to allow them to be members of the club: there was strict segregation in the pub between the members' room and the bar where the players congregated to drink and sing: according to John Nyren, there were several fine singers and instrumentalists among the players. We know, from minutes of meetings and the memories of John Nyren, that prodigious feasting went on in the Bat and Ball during members' meetings. One entry in the minutes of the club recorded: 'A wet day: only three members present: nine bottles of wine'. Members that infringed the rules had to pay fines in the form of wine. And, despite their status in society, the members were not above lewd manners. A minute records that at one dinner the toasts were for:

> *The Queen's Mother*
> *The King*
> *Hambledon Club*
> *Cricket*
> *To the Immortal Memory of Madge*
> *The President*

Madge was the nickname given to the small wicket made up of two stumps. By extension, it was also a vulgar term for a woman's private parts. What fun the members must have had when the shape of the wicket changed and Madge was infiltrated by a third stump. The alteration to the wicket was a result of the brilliant bowling by Hambledon players, Lumpy Stevens in particular. In 1775, when Hambledon played at the Artillery Ground in

London, Stevens was frustrated when he three times beat batsmen with balls that went through the wicket. The club decided this was 'a hard thing upon the bowler' and voted to include a third stump. Other clubs did not immediately follow suit but by the 1780s the wicket composed of three stumps became widespread. The wicket also became taller to accommodate the 'length' or 'lob' bowling perfected by Stevens and David Harris: instead of bowling the ball along the ground, he and other bowlers began to pitch it, so that the ball would rear up at the batsmen and also move to the off or leg side. The ball would often beat the bat and then fly over the wicket. As a result, by 1780 the wicket was almost doubled in height to 22 inches and six inches wide. In 1814 the height and width were increased to 26 inches by eight inches and finally in 1817

*Beach cricket took on a more serious note in 1854 when a match was played on the notorious Goodwin Sands on the Kent coast. The Illustrated London News reported: "The Goodwins, which have been from time immemorial associated with peril and destruction, have just been the scene of exhilarating sport. It appears that on the 10th inst. a party – got up by Mr Morris Thompson, Mr Hammond, and others, at Walmer – visited the Sands for the purpose of playing a game of cricket." The teams were augmented by Captain Pearson and a picked crew of the Spartan, a lugger from Deal. The game started at five in the evening when the players had walked some way along the sands to find a suitable stretch of sand. The game went on until sunset, with the unnamed victors winning by 57 runs.*

*The New Pavillion built at Broadhalfpenny Down.*

to 27 inches by eight inches, which prevail today. To enable batsmen to tackle the new type of bowling, Hambledon player and batmaker John Small designed a new straight blade that not only coped with rising balls but also allowed players to move in the crease and play off front or back foot. The days of clubbing the ball with a curved stick were over. The one major innovation for which Hambledon was not responsible was the move to change the bowler's action. The club outlawed the first attempts at roundarm bowling, which came into effect after Hambledon's decline and was legally replaced in 1864 by overarm bowling: it was a fateful year that saw the first edition of John Wisden's almanack and the first important game in which WG Grace played at the age of 16.

The 1770s and 1780s were glory days for Hambledon. Until the club broke up in 1796, it played 39 matches against All England, of which 23 were victories and one was drawn. Hambledon faced Kent 19 times, winning nine and tying one, and played Surrey in 12 matches, winning four and drawing one. 'All England' is a misnomer and in reality meant players from London and the surrounding counties. It wasn't until the onset of the

industrial revolution in the nineteenth century that cricket expanded into the Midlands and the North. Mill owners founded the Manchester Cricket Club, forerunner of Lancashire CCC, a fact that underscores the shift in power from the old nobility to the new industrialists. Similarly, 'Kent' and 'Surrey' were not true county sides but were made up of players from different clubs within those counties. County cricket proper did not materialise until the late nineteenth century. Nevertheless, the fact that Hambledon was able to take on and frequently beat such powerful sides speaks volumes for the strength of the club and the quality of its players. In 1772 at Broadhalfpenny Down, on 23, 24 and 25 June, Hambledon played England for 500 guineas and won by 53 notches. Hambledon made 146 and 79 and England replied with 109 and 63. John Small scored 78 and 34 in the two Hambledon innings. In the days before boundaries, these were respectable scores. A year later, Hambledon demolished England by an innings and 52 notches at Broadhalfpenny on June 22, 23 and 24. England was bowled out for 122 and 133, while Hambledon made a total of 307, the first recorded occasion when a team scored more than 300. Tom Sueter was top scorer with 67. Hambledon's eminence at this time can seen in the minutes of a meeting in February 1772 that recorded that 'a committee of noblemen and gentlemen of Kent, Hampshire, Surrey, Sussex, Middlesex and London met at the Star and Garter, Pall Mall, and there revised and recorded The Laws of the Noble Game of Cricket'. Hambledon was represented by Philip Dehany, Charles Powlett and Charles Coles and their presence stressed that the club was centrally involved in administering the game.

In 1777, a year after the War of Independence had broken out in the American colonies, Hambledon played their greatest match against All England at Sevenoaks, winning by a decisive innings and 168 runs. Significantly, the game was played with wickets comprised of three stumps and All England were routed despite the presence of Lumpy Stevens in their team, no doubt due to the money he was offered by the Duke of Dorset. They opened the batting, Dorset scoring 0 and 5 and Lumpy 1 and 2, though he carried his bat in the second innings: it must have been an extremely slow knock. Hambledon's impressive total was 403, of which Aylward made 167. The story is told of a waggoner from Farnham who stopped to watch the game at 5pm and saw Aylward defending resolutely against Lumpy Stevens' bowling. Hambledon batted throughout the following day and on the third day the waggoner, on his return journey, was amazed to find Aylward still at the crease. When he was finally bowled out, he had made the highest innings ever recorded in a cricket match.

In 1782 the fateful decision was made to move the club to Windmill Down closer to the village. Richard Nyren followed, leaving the Bat and Ball to take over the George Inn in the High Street, where cricket club meeting and dinners were then held. The move was instigated by the Duke of Dorset on the grounds that Windmill Down was less bleak and offered better facilities for people of quality, who could watch matches from their carriages. He drove the first nail into the coffin of Hambledon cricket. Broadhalfpenny was open common land used for festivals and general merrymaking by the villagers. Windmill, a sign of the changing times, was private land, rented to the club by Farmer Garrett for ten guineas a year. It became

private club property and crowds were restricted, avoiding some of the hoi polloi disliked by Dorset and his entourage. Dorset was soon to leave not just Hambledon but the country when he became the British Ambassador in France. He spent most of his time playing billiards and having affairs, including, it is claimed, one with the Queen of France, Marie Antoinette. He did not break with cricket: he presented Marie Antoinette with a bat and organised a game in the Champs Elysées. He attempted to play a second match during the chaos of the early days of the French Revolution and sent word to Hambledon for players, including Lumpy Stevens, to cross the channel and take part. But as the French nobility headed for the guillotine, Dorset decided to save his neck and hurry back to England.

The wars with Napoleon's France were one reason for Hambledon's decline as a cricketing force. Increased taxation meant the wealthy backers of the game had, for a time, less money to spend on players' wages and gambling. Men of Hampshire were called up for military service to defend the country against an anticipated French invasion and were no longer available to play cricket. The aftermath of the war brought further problems. A series of bad harvests allied to the widespread practice of land enclosure to grow grain and raise cattle and sheep for slaughter brought grinding poverty and unemployment to country areas. Villages became neglected and cottages fell into disrepair while displaced agricultural labourers were forced to seek employment in towns and cities. Early in the nineteenth century, a cricket devotee named WR Weir went to Hambledon and wrote: 'My first visit to this classic region was made on foot from London and I remember I experienced something akin to regret for having travelled so far to see so little. The old Bat and Ball Inn, with its dingy signboard creaking on its rusty hinges as the chill October wind swept over the downs, looked very forlorn, while the landlady was as sour as the beer she tendered me.'

William Cobbett, whose Rural Rides painted a graphic picture of the destruction of the old way of life in the country, visited Hambledon in 1822 and 1826 and also saw the tragic decline of the village and the desperate conditions of many of the inhabitants. He wrote of the countryside in general that the well-fed peasantry of his youth had been replaced by 'a population of starvelings living in hovels and feeding on slops and tea.' Cobbett was a lover of good ale and hated its cheap and narcotic replacement, tea. In Hambledon he noted that the market stall had collapsed while the church, like the village, 'was a tumbledown rubbishy place'. He blamed the village's plight on 'that hellish assemblage' – Portsmouth, Gosport and Southsea – to which many villagers had fled in a vain hope of finding work.

The gravedigger of the cricket club was George Finch, the ninth Earl of Winchilsea. If the Earl of Dorset was a wastrel and a buffoon at least he believed in Hambledon and played for the club. Winchilsea, on the other hand, had no roots in the community and never played for the club, which may have been a benefit as he was an indifferent performer. He was, however, a considerable gambler, often winning as much as £200 in an evening in London clubs and one evening made £840, a fortune by today's standards. Like moths to the flame, landowners were more and more attracted to London, which, as the centre of power and finance and a fast-growing population, offered better opportunities for making money, especially at well-attended sporting events. Winchilsea bet regularly on cricket and his association with Hambledon was simple: he wanted to lure the best players away from the village to the capital. For example, he had spotted the fine batting of 'Silver Billy' Beldham. Beldham recalled working in the fields in 1785 when he saw his employer, Farmer Hilton, in deep conversation with 'a well-dressed gentleman', who turned out to be Winchilsea. After much discussion it was agreed that Beldham would be given time off to go to London to play for Hampshire against All England at White Conduit Fields, a field alongside a pub, long since subsumed into King's Cross Station. Eventually Beldham turned full-time professional and became one of the finest batsmen in the country.

In 1786 Winchilsea joined the club and was elected president, a case no doubt of noblesse oblige. He remained a member of the White Conduit Club, the forerunner of MCC, and he and other members of White Conduit began to pay players for good performances. While Hambledon stagnated, playing only a handful of matches a year against local teams – All England no

## BEER AT THE BAT AND BALL

✱ John Nyren's memory of the quality of the ale or beer sold by his father at the Bat and Ball prompts the questions: what was the beer like and who brewed it? Commercial brewing was growing in the eighteenth century but many publicans, especially in the country, continued to brew on the premises. As the Bat and Ball was originally called the Hut, it must have been a small and rudimentary place, and there may not have been sufficient space to house a small brewery. At least one Hambledon player was a brewer, which indicates that commercial or 'common' brewing was spreading to rural areas. However, John Nyren's strictures against the quality of commercial beer suggest that his father may have found time to brew at the pub. The ale was almost certainly brown in colour. Until the advent of the Industrial Revolution, malt, the basis of beer, was cured or gently roasted over wood fires that produced brown malt. It was not until the turn of the nineteenth century and the invention of coke that malt became lighter in colour and enabled brewers to make pale ale. In London, early in the eighteenth century, a new style of beer emerged known as porter, of which the strongest version was dubbed stout porter, later reduced to stout. Porter, so-called because of its popularity with street-market porters, was an urban drink and it is unlikely that Richard Nyren would have brewed it, let alone had the capacity for the storage vessels needed. His son called his father's beer 'genuine Boniface', which lends credence to the view that Richard did brew his own ale. St Boniface was a Benedictine monk from Devon in the eighth century but in the seventeenth and eighteenth centuries his name was also given to good innkeepers. If Richard Nyren's ale was good enough to be called Boniface, he probably brewed it himself. With plentiful supplies of hops available from Kent and barley malt from East Anglia, his ale would have been biscuity, fruity, bitter and, above all, refreshing.

France where he was elected to the National Assembly. If he had come to Hampshire to watch an unimportant and indifferent cricket match, he ran the risk of being arrested and sent to the gallows as a traitor. The entry in the minutes probably reflects the anger in the village, even among the gentry and the clergy, with government policy that had impoverished the countryside. Far from being a place of rural harmony, Hambledon had long been disputatious and had supported radical or minority causes: parliament during the Civil War, the Swing Riots that smashed agricultural machinery and the Jacobite uprising.

This intriguing reference to Tom Paine in the minutes is the last record of the Hambledon club. It did not fold that year and limped on into the next century, playing occasional games, but its glory days were over. Power had passed to London and MCC. But for a brief period, at a time of tumultuous change in the English countryside, Hambledon, Broadhalfpenny Down and the Bat and Ball pub had combined to bestride the cricketing world like a colossus, refashioning the game and its laws.

We can raise a glass to Hambledon's memory with a song sung in the Bat and Ball and often reproduced in programmes for events on Broadhalfpenny Down today. It was written by the Rev Reynell Cotton, president of the club in 1773, and includes the words:

> *The wickets are pitched now,*
> *and measured the ground,*
> *Then they form a large ring,*
> *and stand gazing around;*
> *Since Ajax fought Hector,*
> *in sight of all Troy,*
> *No contest was seen with*
> *such fear and such joy.*
>
> *Then fill up your glass,*
> *he's the best who drinks most.*
> *Here's the Hambledon Club! –*
> *who refuses the toast?*
> *Let's join in the praise of the*
> *bat and the wicket,*
> *And sing in full chorus*
> *the patrons of cricket.*

longer came calling – many of its players went to London to play for fees that, at a time of unemployment and rural poverty, were attractive and much-needed. In 1786 White Conduit played a combined Kent and Surrey team and among the White Conduit players were Small, Mann, Walker and others from Hambledon. Later that summer when White Conduit played Kent at Bishopsbourne the team included no fewer than six Hambledon men. The die, in every way, had been cast.

The last weekly meeting of the Hambledon club was held on 29 August 1796. A handful of members and their guests were in the clubhouse while a match went on outside on Windmill Down. It was a sad sign of Hambledon's decline that, in order to take on Portsmouth, the 'Hambledon' team included players from clubs in Petersfield and East Meon. In the clubhouse, the minutes record that among those present was 'Mr Thomas Paine, author of The Rights of Man.' This is almost certainly a spoof. Paine, the leading radical of the time, had a price on his head. He had gone to America to support the revolution against Britain and from there had gone to

# BEER AND SKITTLES:
## *The first-class grounds and the best pubs*

# LORD'S
(MCC and Middlesex)

## MARYLEBONE CRICKET CLUB
Lord's Ground, St John's Wood Road, London, NW8 8QN

☎ (020) 7289 1611 for general enquiries
(020) 7616 8603 for prospects of play
www.lords.org/www.middlesexccc.com
Email: reception@mcc.org.uk/middx@middlesexccc.com
*See the Lord's website for email addresses for different functions, such as media, tours etc*

### Getting There
Lord's is five minutes' walk from St John's Wood Underground Station
on the Jubilee Line.
**For buses** see www.tfl.gov.uk or telephone (020) 7222 1234

Lord's has pomp. It is more than just the most famous cricket ground
in the world, it's a revered sporting institution. Australians, with a
well-honed dislike of Pommy patrician attitudes, nevertheless admit to a
shiver down the spine when they enter the ground through the Grace
Gates, or step on to the springy turf to play. Even Americans, who have
lost all knowledge of a game that once vied with baseball for popularity
in their country, have heard of the ground, though they think it has some
connection with the House of Lords. American friends sit in my garden
with a degree of respect and even awe on a wooden bench, numbered
in stencilled green from 537 to 540, bought when the old Mound Stand
was demolished – seats so uncomfortable that spectators had to hire
cushions for a tanner (sixpence) a day to avoid getting creases and
splinters in a delicate part of the anatomy.

Thomas Lord was not lordly. He was a jobbing entrepreneur, but
there were aristocratic origins to the ground that carries his name.
Lord Winchilsea, who had picked up the game when he was at school at
Eton, his friend the Honourable Colonel Charles Lennox (nephew of the
Duke of Richmond), and other members of London's high society met
regularly in a Pall Mall tavern called the Star & Garter. The cricketers
among them started to play regularly from the mid-1780s at the White
Conduit Club attached to White Conduit House in Islington, an imposing
name but in reality a pub. But Winchilsea and his fellow nobles were
unhappy with a venue that attracted large, noisy crowds including many
'undesirables' such as thieves, beggars and prostitutes. In 1787,
Winchilsea and Lennox provided the cash for Thomas Lord to build a new
ground at Dorset Square, close to Baker Street and Marylebone Road.

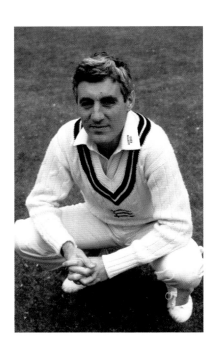

*Right, Mike Brearley OBE, captained England in 31 out of 39 of the Test matches that he played.*

*Below, Middlesex's Patsy Hendren (centre) holds the record for the highest individual innings for MCC.*

*Opposite page, Fred Titmus also played football professionally for Watford.*

### GREAT FEATS

☆ For MCC, the highest innings total was 607 against Cambridge University in 1902, and the lowest total was 27 against Yorkshire in the same year – from hubris to nemesis in one season. Patsy Hendren holds the record for the highest individual innings for MCC: 214 against Yorkshire in 1926, while the highest partnership is 301 scored by Dennis Amiss and Mike Brearley against Leicestershire in 1976.

☆ Among the great bowling performances, AEE Vogler took 9 for 44 in an innings against the West Indies in 1906.

☆ For Middlesex, the highest innings total for the county is 612 for 8 declared against Notts in 1921, while the highest individual innings is, again, Patsy Hendren with 277 not out against Kent in 1922. The best bowling performance in an innings is by Gubby Allen, who took all 10 wickets for 40 against Lancashire in 1929.

Lord's family came from Yorkshire but had moved to Norfolk when their devotion to the Roman Catholic faith made life uncomfortable. Thomas left Norfolk for London, found work as a steward and groundsman at the White Conduit and bowled in matches there. He was later to build a successful wine business and dabble in property, but first he accepted the challenge to create a new cricket ground. He fenced the site, charged sixpence admission and also sold alcohol to spectators. The first match was played there in 1787 and a year later a new club, formed from the leading players at White Conduit, adopted the name of MCC – the Marylebone Cricket Club. Thomas Lord moved on when he couldn't afford the lease at Dorset Square: property prices were soaring in London and the landlord demanded a ruinous rent for the ground. Lord created a new ground at the North Bank in St John's Wood, taking with him the turf from his previous venue. He was soon forced to move again when the Regent's Canal was dug on a course that would have taken it straight through the ground. Lord's third and final move in 1813 was to a former duck pond on the St John's Wood Estate rented from the Eyre family. The choice of land was fortuitous, given the agony and infamy of the term duck for batsmen. Once again, Lord took his turf with him. He put a high fence round the land and built a pavilion and a tavern: the latter, in an act of vandalism, was torn down in the 1960s. In 1814 the first game was played there between MCC and Hertfordshire, which MCC won by a resounding innings and 27 runs. The scorecard for the match makes interesting reading, emphasising the class disparity between the two sides. Most of the Herts players are listed only by their surnames, whereas the MCC are all 'Mr', signifying amateurs, with the exception of two Honourables, Kinnaird and Bligh, and Lord Frederick Beauclerk, who made six hundred guineas a year from gambling on cricket.

In 1825, Lord sold the ground for £5,000 to William Ward, a member of MCC, director of the Bank of England and a member of Parliament. Lord continued his wine and other businesses before retiring to Hampshire where he died in 1832 aged 76. His

cricket ground could have been renamed Ward's but it fortunately retained the title that assured Thomas's legacy.

The homespun democracy of Hambledon, where ennobled landowners mixed with the gentry, farmers and farm labourers, did not transfer to London. A revised and updated version of the laws of the game was produced by MCC just one year after the club was founded. The laws, it was recorded, were a revision of those drawn up by a committee of 'Noblemen and Gentlemen of Kent, Hampshire, Surrey, Sussex, Middlesex and London' at a meeting in the Star & Garter. Lumpy Stevens need not apply.

I have posed the question: Why Hambledon? A second question arises: Why MCC? There were scores, if not hundreds, of cricket clubs in London and the surrounding counties. Why did one of them become so celebrated that it acquired the unchallenged right to control the laws of the game and to become its ruling authority? The club's position, in a sylvan area of north-west London but shortly to be well served by the new train services, helped, but the main reason was the awe with which MCC quickly surrounded itself. Noblemen ran the club and they fielded sides composed of amateurs and gentlemen, disdaining to use professionals unless they were short of 11 men. The English, the new

*Right,
A bench seat
from the old
Mound Stand at
Lord's, now in
the author's garden.*

middle class in particular, were anxious to tug a forelock in the direction of their betters and hurried to join a club that became so dominant that it had no need of the definite article: it was simply MCC. By the turn of the century, the club had produced two further revisions of the laws. It was inviolable.

Untouchable, it got away with providing a poor pitch, which was cropped by sheep until the lawn mower was invented. The area in front of what became the Mound Stand was covered with small ponds, which were bricked in and then covered with turf when the ground was extended. Surrey and Sussex both refused to play there in the 1850s as they deemed the ground to be below standard. Observers marvelled when WG Grace, aged 19, scored 134 out of a total of 201 when the Gentlemen played the Players at Lord's in 1868 on a pitch, according to one observer, 'covered with rough grass wetted and rolled down'. A few years later, the club relayed the entire ground, but two of Lord's shortcomings remain to this day. One is the slope: from the Grandstand to the Tavern Stand, the ground falls by six feet six inches. Sir Pelham 'Plum' Warner, who has his own stand named after him, described the extent of

the slope as being 'about the height of a tall man in a top hat'. Surely only at Lord's would such a description be made. The slope still remains, as does the infamous ridge at the Nursery End, where the ball occasionally shoots or keeps unnaturally low. The ridge was flattened but has mysteriously reappeared again in recent years, along with a second, smaller ridge at the Pavilion End. Theories abound to explain these curious phenomena: the presence of old drains under the ground, or the ceaseless pounding of bowlers' boots on the most-used pitches in the country are two of them.

Lord's had other problems in the nineteenth century. A fire in 1825 destroyed the pavilion and all its contents, including scorebooks and other priceless records. A second pavilion was built and that was replaced in 1890 by the celebrated redbrick one with its white picket fence and balconies, topped by the cupola with the wrought-iron, imperious and entwined letters of MCC.

There was also a re-run of the threat to Lord's, this time not from the Regent's Canal but the proposed Great Central Railway, which wanted to buy the land in order to drive a line through it to a station at Marylebone. A Bill was presented to parliament in 1888 but it was rejected and the company had to dig a tunnel deep under the cricket ground – another cause for the ridge, perhaps. Cricket was now the national game and the greensward could not be touched by the iron way.

The railway, nevertheless, was a potent symbol of the new Britain created by the Industrial Revolution. It was factory owners, not land owners, who now held sway. William Nicholson, who had made a fortune from gin distilling, funded the new pavilion at Lord's with a loan of £21,000. London and other towns and cities were growing fast, and large crowds swarmed to cricket matches and other leisure pursuits. The likes of Lord Harris and Lord Hawke would continue to be the voice of English cricket into the early part of the twentieth century, but the nobility's influence was waning. As early as 1877, MCC recognised the growing popularity of county cricket and invited Middlesex, founded in 1864, to base itself at Lord's. The professionals, players who did not warrant a first name or a

'Mr' on the scorecard, had stormed the citadel. With due deference to their landlord, however, Middlesex always had several amateurs in their sides until the distinction between 'gentleman' and 'player' was swept away in the 1960s, though not before there was a celebrated announcement at Lord's of a correction to the scorecard: 'For FJ Titmus read Titmus FJ'. Players by this time were allowed to have initials on the card, but only gentlemen had them in front of their surnames. In spite of loyal service to both England and Middlesex, Fred Titmus was judged not to be a gent.

A century after Middlesex came to play at Lord's, and not without a touch of irony, MCC was forced to ask the county club to play some matches away from St John's Wood. The ground has 18 wickets but they were in such demand as a result of Test matches, One-Day Internationals, sundry cup finals and other regular fixtures that the pitches were suffering from over-use. The Middlesex diaspora was not the only change at

*Left,*
*During a break*
*in a game,*
*children play*
*Kwik cricket.*

Lord's. In spite of a reputation for being deeply conservative, MCC and its associated bodies have reinvented themselves on a number of occasions. Early in the twentieth century, the Board of Control for Test Matches, the Advisory County Cricket Committee and the Imperial Cricket Conference were set up and based at Lord's to administer the domestic and international aspects of the game. In 1968, MCC created the Test and County Cricket Board (TCCB) to run the professional game while the new Cricket Council became the governing body of the sport. The council was in effect a front organisation for MCC. As MCC is a private club, it cannot accept public funds, whereas the council was able to get financial support from the government. One chairman of the TCCB was George Mann, who played for England and Middlesex and was a director of the large brewing group Watney Mann & Truman. In the 1990s the structure changed again with the creation of the ECB, the England and Wales Cricket Board, which took over the responsibilities of the TCCB, the National Cricket Council (which runs the game at grassroots level, including schools), and the Cricket Council. In case anyone should ask what there is left for MCC to do, the answer is to foster the game at all levels and to send teams to countries that either play the game or, it is hoped, will do so in future. In 1982, for example, an MCC side played 11 games in the United States and included such former Test players as Tony Lewis, Fred Titmus, John Jameson and Mushtaq Mohammed.

The ground has seen profound changes. With the exception of the pavilion, all other areas have been altered out of all recognition, most notably the new Mound Stand topped by a fleet of flying saucer shapes and the imposing Media Centre, designed by Jan Kaplicky and winner of a Royal Institute of British Architects Award, at the Nursery End. The Nursery, it should be noted, is so-called not because it nurtures young cricketing talent but because it was once an agricultural market. The cruel nickname for the Media Centre, with an allusion to the mouth of the wife of a leading politician, will be left to the reader's imagination.

Lords Cricket Ground and the world-famous media centre designed by Jan Kaplicky.

# THE TOUR

Lord's has long since thrown off its reputation for stuffiness. Today the gates are thrown open and all are warmly welcomed. The tour of the ground is handled superbly, with wit as well as knowledge, and nothing is off limits. The Long Room in the pavilion, over 28 metres long by 8 metres wide, has portraits, some in oil, of cricketing heroes, including Billy Beldham, Thomas Lord, Alfred Mynn, George Parr and John Wisden from the early days of the game and, within touching distance of modern times, Gubby Allen, Don Bradman, Douglas Jardine and 'Plum' Warner. There is the much-copied painting of four young Nottingham chimney-sweeps 'Tossing for Innings' and Francis Hayman's image of cricket at St Mary-le-Bone Fields in 1740. A stupendous collection of bats allows visitors to follow the development of the implement, from a curved one used in 1750 to an early straight one from 1774, to those owned and wielded by WG Grace, Alfred Mynn and Fuller Pilch. Grace's bat was the one he used when he made his highest score of 334 for MCC against Kent in 1876. Jack Hobbs's bat served to make his final century, while Wilfred Rhodes's willow was the one he carried in his partnership with George Hirst at the Oval in 1902 against the Australians, when Hirst famously told his partner 'We'll get 'em in singles, Wilfred'. A smaller room off the Long Room is used to greet and give tea to the Queen when she visits Lord's, usually to welcome the home and touring sides during a Test Match. Visitors are then taken to see the players' dressing rooms

that contain an honours board listing great achievements with bat and ball.

Opposite the rear of the pavilion, at the end of a complex of buildings that includes a shop, the library, and squash and Real Tennis courts, the museum is a spacious series of rooms that tracks the history of cricket over 400 years, and includes collections of paintings of cricket

grounds throughout the world, club cricket ties, a pair of Don Bradman's boots (he had small feet, size six) and photographs of players down the centuries. One of the most curious artefacts in any museum must be the ball surmounted by a stuffed sparrow that records the occasion in 1936 when Jehangir Khan, playing in a MCC versus Cambridge match, killed the unfortunate bird in mid-flight as he bowled to TN Pearce. But the centrepiece of the museum is formed by the Ashes Urn, surprisingly small and described by

Geoffrey Moorhouse as 'no bigger than a large brown egg cup', and the Wisden Trophy, fought for with great tenacity by England and Australia. The Urn always remains at Lord's, but the resting place of the Wisden Trophy is determined by the result of each Ashes series. According to Moorhouse, in his marvellous book Lord's, there is a rumour that the Ashes Urn is empty as a result of a diligent cleaning woman disposing of the contents back in 1883. Perish the thought.

From the museum, visitors are taken on a tour of the stands and finally into the Media Centre, with its impressive view of the ground and where the once urgent clatter of typewriters has been replaced by the more subdued click of computer keys.

Tours of the ground take place every day except when major matches are being played or the ground is being prepared. Between April and September, tours are held at 10am, 12 noon and 2pm; on other match days only the 10am tour can enter the Pavilion. Between October and March, tours are at 12 noon and 2pm.

2006 prices were £8 for an adult, child £5, seniors and students £6. There are special rates for group and educational tours.

For further information, including up-to-date prices, contact:
☎ (020) 7616 8595/6;
fax (020) 7266 3825
**Email:** tours@mcc.org.uk

*Above, The four-inch-high Ashes Urn, on display in Sydney, Australia during the lead up to the 2006 Ashes series.*

## Recommended Pubs
## LONDON

### STAR
38 St John's Wood Terrace, NW8 6LS

☼ 11-11; 12-10.30 Sun
☎ (020) 7722 1051
⊖ St John's Wood (Jubilee Line)

The Star is the closest pub to Lord's and is handy for the Underground station. It is a comfortable and welcoming community local where a Toby Jug logo on the exterior signals that the long defunct London brewer, Charrington, once owned it. There is wood-panelling by the yard, mirrors and a large fireplace topped by books at one end and surrounded by photographs of old movie stars, including Fred Astaire and Cary Grant. The opposite end has generous seating, including wall settles, a cabinet with a collection of glass and china, and paintings with a seagoing theme. A small back room has a sporting theme, mainly devoted to horseracing but with photographs of George Best and Mohammed Ali. The pub is dominated by a vast wooden bar held up by wooden pillars and a beam. The beers are Draught Bass and Worthington Bitter.

### WARRINGTON HOTEL
93 Warrington Crescent, W9

☼ 11-11; 12-10.30 Sun
☎ (020) 7286 0310/2229
⊖ Warwick Avenue or Maida Vale (Bakerloo Line)

The Warrington, which is no longer a hotel, is just a short walk from Lord's on the other side of Maida Vale Road. It is worth the stroll as this is one of London's most amazing pubs with the unique history of being a Church of England-owned Victorian brothel. Today the upstairs rooms are used as a Thai restaurant, while the main bar and entrance form a shrine to Art Nouveau. Originally built in 1859, The Warrington was rebuilt in 1900 during a boom in speculative pub building in London. The ornate entrance has two large domed lights, while the main room has marbled pillars, a marble surround fireplace, leaded windows, and an astonishing decorated canopy above the bar. The risqué past can be seen in the statuettes of naked women holding aloft lights in wall alcoves. The side bar is positively sedate after the main room's pomp, with wood-panelled walls and Art Nouveau lamps on the bar. The Warrington was bought by the celebrated chef Gordon Ramsay in 2006 and will be known as The London Bar. The first floor will house a full restaurant and selected items will be available in the pub.

## WARWICK CASTLE
6 Warwick Place, W9 2PX

🕑 11-11; 12-10.30 Sun
☎ (020) 7432 1331
🚇 Warwick Avenue

The Warwick is just a short walk from the station and down
a narrow road that looks like a cul-de-sac but which does
lead into a further road. This is the area known as Little
Venice, bordered by the Regent's Canal and with magnificent aristocratic houses. The pub sign shows, unsurprisingly,
the image of Warwick Castle: the earls of Warwick owned
tracts of land in the area. It is a delightful wood-panelled
pub with engraved windows and a large horseshoe bar
topped by a moulded gantry. There is a Bass mirror on one
wall and a large fireplace with a painting of Paddington railway station in the nineteenth century above it. At the back of
the main bar is a small room, while to the left of the bar, a
further room has folding doors that create a café atmosphere
on a warm day along with the extensive seating on the
pavement. The beers are Adnams Broadside and Greene
King IPA and Abbot. The menu, available at lunchtime and
in the evening, includes lasagne, chilli, fish and chips,
steaks, bangers and mash, vegetarian burger, jacket potatoes, ploughman's and salads, with a roast on Sunday.

## ONE THAT GOT AWAY

## CROCKER'S FOLLY
24 Aberdeen Place, London, NW8.

This amazing pub was the closest to Lord's but is currently
boarded up and derelict. It was built in the nineteenth
century by a speculative builder called Frank Crocker, who
thought Marylebone Station would be built over the road.
He lavished money on his rococo masterpiece, only to find
that the station had been built a mile further down the
road. Crocker went bust and the pub, called the Crown,
was nicknamed Crocker's Folly. The name was formally
adopted some years ago. I have many happy memories of
the place, including the first day of the Centenary Test at
Lord's when, after an hour, the heavens opened and I,
accompanied by a few thousand others, spent the rest of
the day in Crocker's.

## Other Cricket Grounds and Recommended Pubs

Middlesex also plays at Richmond, Shenley, Southgate and Uxbridge.

### RICHMOND

**RICHMOND CRICKET CLUB**
The Pavilion
Old Deer Park, 187 Kew Road
Richmond, TW9 2AZ

☎ (020) 8332 6696
(including prospects of play)

**Red Cow**
59 Sheen Road, TW9 1YJ

✺ 11-11.30; 12-10.30 Sun
☎ (020) 8940 2511

**Beer:** Young's Bitter, Special and seasonal beers.

### SHENLEY

**SHENLEY CRICKET CENTRE**
The Pavilion
The Denis Compton Oval
Radlett Lane, Shenley,
Herts, WD7 9DW

☎ (01923) 859022
(including prospects of play)

**Red Lion**
78-80 Watling Street
Radlett, Herts, WD7 7NP

✺ 11-midnight; 12-11.30 Sun
☎ (01923) 855341.
Opposite Radlett railway station; accommodation available.
**Beer:** Young's Bitter, Special and seasonal beers.

### SOUTHGATE

**SOUTHGATE CRICKET CLUB**
The Walker Cricket Ground
Waterfall Road, Southgate
London, N14 7JZ

☎ (020) 8886 8381
(including prospects of play)

**New Crown**
80-84 Chase Side
Southgate, London, N14 5PH

✺ 11-11; 12-10.30 Sun

**Beer:** Courage Best and Directors, Greene King Abbot and Shepherd Neame Spitfire.

In the area:
**Winchmore Hill Cricket Club**
The Paulin Ground
Ford's Grove, N21 3ER

✺ 7 (12 Sat)-11; 12-10.30 Sun
(closes 6pm in winter)

Visitors admitted on production of CAMRA membership card or copy of the Good Beer Guide.

**Beer:** Greene King IPA and guest beers.

### UXBRIDGE

**UXBRIDGE CRICKET CLUB**
The Pavilion
Gatting Way, Park Road
Uxbridge, Middlesex, UB8 1NR

☎ (01895) 237571
(including prospects of play)

**Load of Hay**
33 Villier Streeet, UB8 2PU

✺ 11-11.30; 12-11.30 Sun
☎ (01895) 234676

**Beer:** Fuller's London Pride and guest beers.

# DERBYSHIRE

## DERBYSHIRE COUNTY CRICKET CLUB

Nottingham Road,
Derby,
DE21 6DA

☎ (01332) 388101 (general enquiries)
(01332) 383211 (prospects of play)
**www**.derbyshireccc.com
**Email:** sue.evans@derbyshireccc.com

### Getting there

**Derby Midland train station** is a mile and a quarter from the ground.
From the station Trent Buses 29 or Derby City buses 42, 43, 44, 45,
46 and 47 go to the ground.
Entry is via either the Pentagon Island gates or from Sir Frank Whittle Way,
named after the Derby engineer who invented the jet engine

Even the most fervent Derbyshire supporter would claim that the ground, for most of its history, was the most attractive in the country. For years, it was made up of a pavilion, the cricket area and rudimentary seating, with the rest a virtual wasteland. The ground started life as the Derby Racecourse and was known as the Racecourse Ground until early this century when it became the County Cricket Ground. Until the old buildings were demolished in 2001 and 2002, the racing element dominated here, with the players even using the old jockeys' quarters as changing rooms. Since then, there has been rapid development of the entire ground with the main Lund Pavilion, which dates from the 1980s, joined by sponsors' suites, a new scoreboard, the Don Arnott and Steetley stands, a supporters' room and club shop, an indoor school and new and much-needed seating. Thanks to a vigorous tree-planting programme, funded in part by Derby County FC, the entire ground is now far more agreeable and much changed from the 1980s when I saw Viv Richards, playing here for Somerset, score a century in even time, watched by a 'crowd' that could have been accommodated in a handful of telephone boxes.

As well as horse racing, the ground was also used by Derby County FC until the club moved to the Baseball Ground in 1894. One FA Cup Final was played at the Racecourse as well as five semi-finals. The ground, opened in 1848 for racing, was first used for cricket in 1863 by South Derbyshire CC. The club played and defeated the first-ever touring side, the Australian Aborigines, in 1868. Floodlighting has been installed for day/night and Twenty20 matches and the ground now has a capacity of 9,500. It is not a Test ground, but One Day Internationals, including New Zealand versus Pakistan in the 1999 World Cup, are staged here. Disappointingly, for a club with a long and fascinating history, it has no museum or any exhibition showing famous players, teams, trophies or equipment.

*Right,
Stan Worthington
played for Derbyshire
in the 1930s and
hit 238 runs in an
innings in 1937.*

*Below right,
Former Derbyshire
captain Kim Barnett.*

## GREAT FEATS

✷ The highest innings total for the county is 645, scored against Hampshire in 1898, while the highest individual innings score for the county is TS Worthington's 238 against Sussex in 1937.

✷ Former captain Kim Barnett has taken part in two remarkable partnerships: 417 with TW Tweats against Yorkshire in 1997 and with John Morris 221 against Northants in 1986.

✷ The best bowling performance in an innings for the county was 9 for 39 by GA Davidson against Warwickshire in 1895, while the best bowling performance in a match was 14 for 100 by G Porter against Hampshire in the same year

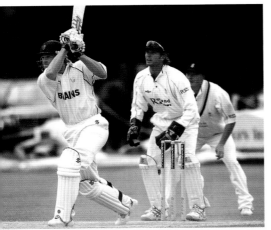

*Left,
Glamorgan batsman
Michael Powell
hits his opening ball
over the bowlers
head, watched
by Derbyshire
wicketkeeper captain
Luke Sutton,
during third day of
a Fizzell County
Championship game
at the County
Ground, Derby*

*Left,
Groundskeepers
pulling a tarpaulin
over the playing
area during
heavy rain.*

## Recommended Pubs
## DERBY

### ALEXANDRA HOTEL
203 Siddals Roads, DE1 2QE

🕐 11-11; 12-3; 7-10.30 Sun
☎ (01332) 293993

'The Alex' is named after the Danish princess who married the Prince of Wales, later Edward VII, in 1863. It began life as the Midland Coffee House and later, as a pub, was owned by Shipstone's of Nottingham and Bateman's of Wainfleet before passing to Tynemill of Nottingham. Tynemill is owned by Chris Holmes, national chairman of CAMRA in the late 1970s, who now runs 17 pubs in the East Midlands with a fierce dedication to cask beer. Holmes serves more cask beers in a year than any other pub group. The Alex, in common with the rest of the group's pubs, offers beers from Castle Rock, Tynemill's Nottingham brewery, but managers are free to buy in guest beers from other craft breweries. The Alex offers Castle Rock's Elsie Mo, Harvest Pale and seasonal beers, with such guests as Bateman's XB, Marston's Pedigree and Timothy Taylor's Landlord. There is a fine choice of Belgian ales and genuine continental lagers, draught cider and around a dozen malt whiskies. The large public bar has ample seating on varnished floorboards while the walls are decorated with railway memorabilia: the lounge bar is both quieter and more plush. The pub is just a short walk from the railway station and an even shorter stagger from the Brunswick (see next entry). Filled rolls are available at lunchtime and there is a roast on Sunday. The Alex offers excellent accommodation that is popular with those attending both the cricket ground and Derby County football ground: it is advisable to book in advance.

Q ✿ 🛏 ◑ ◗ 🍴 ♿ ⇌ 🚌 ♣🍸 P

*The Derby branch of CAMRA, founded in the Alexandra Tavern in 1974, stages one of the best annual regional beer festivals. It is conveniently held in July during the cricket season and adds to beer drinking delights in the city. www.derbycamra.org.uk*

## BRUNSWICK INN
1 Railway Terrace, DE1 2RU

✪ 11-11; 12-10.30 Sun
☎ (01332) 290677

This is more than a wonderful pub, it is a piece of Victorian history, a fascinating example of nineteenth-century paternalism. The wedge-shaped, end-of-terrace building forms part of a small estate of houses built in the 1840s by the Midland Railway for its employees and designed by the architect Francis Thompson. The estate fell into disrepair after World War Two and was saved by Derby Civic Society in the 1970s. The society restored the buildings and won Grade II listing for them. In 1987 the pub was bought by Trevor Harris and John Evans who discovered that it originally had bore holes to provide water for a small brewery: in other words, it had been a nineteenth-century brewpub. Trevor and John restored the link by building a 10-barrel brewery that supplies the Brunswick and, as its fame spread, other pubs in the area. Trevor and John eventually went their separate ways – Trevor now runs the Derby Brewery in Nottingham Road not far from the cricket ground – and the pub was bought by Everards Brewery of Leicester. Nothing has been changed: the pub's brewery continues to produce a wide range of delicious beers and the intimate charm of the inn, with its many rooms, remains

intact. The beers include Triple Hop, Second Brew, Railway Porter, Old Accidental, Triple Gold and Father Mike's, the last named after a local priest. There are also many seasonal and occasional brews and guest beers from other breweries and a total of 15 handpumps. You can enjoy your beer in the spacious bar area that leads off the corridor from the entrance or in either of the side rooms with settles, flagstone floors and coal fires. The brewery can be seen beyond these rooms at the end of the corridor. There is a further downstairs room to the right that narrows to the apex of the wedge, while an upstairs room is reserved for lunchtime diners.

This marvellous and unique pub, voted Derby CAMRA's pub of the year in 2004, is just a couple of minutes' walk from Derby railway station and is the perfect place for a beer before and after a visit to the cricket ground. Don't miss it.

Q ☇ ✪ ◗ ♿ ⇄ 🚌 🍎 ♨

## OLDE DOLPHIN INNE
5a Queen Street, DE1 3DL

✪ 10.30-midnight; 12-11 Sun
☎ (01332) 267711

Derby's oldest pub dates from 1530 and stands almost at the foot of the immense Gothic tower of the city's cathedral. The timber-framed and heavily beamed pub is a step back in time, with several small bars and snugs linked by a passageway, each with its own entrance. You get the feeling that it was designed to allow drinkers to escape from the police, press gangs or wives angry that the weekly wages were being washed down husbands' throats. There are flagstone floors, leaded windows, open coal fires, polished wall benches and tables with cast-iron frames, and memorabilia of old Derby hangs on the panelled walls. The pub stages regular Olde English Roasts, meals that include a tour of the cellars, which have a grisly history. In the eighteenth century, a young doctor staying at the inn arranged for two body-snatchers to deliver the body of a young woman. The doctor took the body to the cellar under the lounge and started to dissect her. Suddenly the woman came to, jumped up and ran screaming around the cellar, clutching her entrails, until she collapsed and died. The shock was so great that the doctor's hair turned white. His family hushed up the scandal but had him committed to a lunatic asylum. The Dolphin also boasts several ghosts, including a Scotsman dressed in full Highland regalia, a Blue Lady who walks through walls and is reputed to have had an affair with the highwayman Dick Turpin, and a young child who is seen on the stairs leading up to the restaurant. It's a pub where you will need a stiff drink. In keeping with the atmosphere of the place, there is no piped music to interrupt conversation and newspapers are provided for those who wish to catch up with the news or the cricket scores. It is a haven for cask beer drinkers with 10 handpumps dispensing beer from regional and small brewers. On a recent visit, it was fitting that Bowler, from the Langton Brewery in Leicestershire, which started life at the Bell Inn opposite Langton Cricket Club's ground, was on offer, along with Adnams, Black Sheep, Deuchars IPA, Marston's Pedigree and several guest beers. The pub stages a beer festival every July. Good value bar food is complemented by a steak restaurant upstairs that has the air of an old London chop house. There is also a beer garden at the back of the pub, the ideal place to enjoy a pint on hazy, lazy spring and summer days.

## DURHAM

### DURHAM COUNTY CRICKET CLUB
County Ground
Riverside, Chester-le-Street, Co Durham, DH3 3QR

☎ (0191) 387 1717 (including prospects of play)
www.durhamccc.co.uk
Email reception@durham.co.uk

### Getting There
Chester-le-Street railway station is one mile from the ground. It's a case of walking or taking a cab from the taxi office at the station. To reach the ground on foot, walk down the road and turn right at the first junction. Go over a mini roundabout and at the next roundabout turn left down Ropery Lane: you will pass another cricket ground, Chester-le-Street CC, on the left behind a high wall. At the next roundabout, cross the road and the Riverside ground faces you.

You can tell you're in the far north for, among its other distinctions, the Riverside is the only first-class ground to have its own brass band. They'll find fast bowlers down coalmines next. The band has taken part in the annual Brass Band Championships and concerts are staged at the ground. The Riverside's greater claim to fame is that Durham was given first-class status in 1991, the first county to be so awarded for 70 years. It was a status that was long overdue: Durham were Minor Counties champions nine times between 1900 and 1984, and achieved the remarkable distinction of being the first minor county to defeat a first-class county in the Gillette Cup in 1973, when they overcame mighty Yorkshire. Finally, between 1976 and 1982, Durham played 65 minor county matches without suffering a single defeat, a record that still stands and is likely to do so for some considerable time.  As a result of this prodigious record, the county club committee applied for first-class status and it was granted by the Test and County Cricket Board two years later.

In spite of attracting such cricketing luminaries as Ian Botham (who ended his illustrious career at Durham), Wayne Larkins and Dean Jones, the club led a peripatetic existence for its first few years as a first-class county. It played at Chester-le-Street CC, Darlington (which is still used as a second ground), Durham, Gateshead, Hartlepool, Newcastle and Stockton-on-Tees. In 1993 the club was granted planning permission to build a new ground at the Riverside in a superb location overlooked by the imposing bulk of the 700-year-old Lumley Castle and close to the River Wear. The aim was for facilities that would attract Test and international

matches to the area. Financial support was provided by the EU, the Sports Council and the Forestry Commission. The ground was ready for cricket in 1993 but further work continued, with the final phase, the opening of the Don Robson Pavilion, conducted by the Queen in October 1996.

The ground is impressively modern with no attempt at faux Victorian. The playing area is the second largest in the country: its capacity is currently 15,000 but this will grow to 22,000. As well as cricket, the complex has facilities for football and athletics, and there is a wildlife area and a park. The historic opening first-class match at the Riverside was in May 1995, when Warwickshire, rather unsportingly, beat the home team. In 1999, World Cup matches were staged there and a year later the club hosted One Day internationals, with the first Test staged in 2003. The granting of Test status to Durham was not without controversy, as several older first-class counties that have never enjoyed Test status felt snubbed, though most of them do not have the crowd capacity that the Riverside offers. Today, the club enjoys international recognition, with Paul Collingwood and Steve Harmison being regular members of the England Test squad. The Australian David Boon, who played for Durham for a few seasons, also won international recognition, but for his extra-curricular activities as well as his famously pugna-

*Above,*
*Mexican wave*
*Below left,*
*Australian-born*
*Dean Jones, a former*
*Derbyshire captain.*

*Below centre,*
*Durham's Steve*
*Harmison, a regular*
*member of*
*the England*
*Test squad.*

*Below right,*
*Durham's Paul*
*Collingwood holds*
*the record for the*
*highest individual*
*innings for the county.*

## GREAT FEATS

✼ The highest innings total for the county is 485 for 3 against Durham University in 2001. The highest individual innings for the county is 190 by Paul Collingwood against Sri Lanka in 2002. In 2001, JJB Lewis and ML Love scored 258 against Nottinghamshire.

✼ SJE Brown holds the best bowling performance for the county in an innings: 7 for 51 by against Lancashire in 2000, while the best bowling performance in a match is 11 for 192 by the same bowler against Warwickshire in 1995.

cious batting. He once consumed 52 cans of lager on a flight from London to Sydney and was dubbed 'the keg on legs'. When he retired from cricket, Boon appeared in a television promotion in Australia during 2005 and 2006 for Victoria Bitter (actually a lager), titled Boonanza. Suitably impressed, his home state of Tasmania has named 15 November a public holiday called David Boon Day. Drinking is obligatory.

Austin's Bar and Bistro at the Riverside is notable for two reasons: it offers some fascinating memorabilia and also serves a cask beer, Greene King's Old Speckled Hen. The bar, named after Arthur Austin, a former player and club patron, is open to the general public, not just members, and it has photos of former players and teams. There is a portrait of Don Bradman, who was an external patron of the club, and a collection of signed team bats from many countries, including Australia, India, New Zealand, Pakistan and Sri Lanka. The members' dining room in the pavilion has display cabinets of more signed bats, trophies, and team and player photos as well as the Denis Compton Award for the year's most promising young cricketer.

Lumley Castle, which looms over the ground, is reputed to be haunted and when the touring Australian team stayed there one player ran screaming from his room during the night, saying he had seen a ghost, and demanding to sleep in another room already occupied by a team mate. It is comforting to know that even the Aussies have a Big Girl's Blouse among their number.

## Recommended Pubs
## CHESTER-LE-STREET

### BUTCHERS ARMS
Middle Chare (off Front Street), DH3 3QD

✪ 11-3; 6.30-11 (11am-midnight Thur & Fri);
12-4; 6.30-10.30 Sun
☎ (0191) 388 3605
www.4durhamcounty.co.uk/pubs

From the cricket ground, walk back into town and turn right into Front Street. Walk down the street until you reach Middle Chare, on the right. The Butchers Arms dominates the road with its brick built exterior decked with carriage lamps. It is a true community local with a room for meetings and well-appointed accommodation, which makes it a good venue if you are visiting the cricket ground and need to stay overnight. It's also a good base for visiting Beamish Museum and the Angel of the North sculpture at Gateshead. The Butchers has a deserved reputation for its food, the highpoints of which are fresh fish and speciality pies. The pub's dedication to good beer can be measured by the collection of pump clips behind the bar. As well as regular Cameron's Strongarm, Jenning's Cumberland Ale and Marston's Pedigree, the pub has a rolling programme of guest beers, with three new beers every fortnight.

✿ 🍺 ◑ ⇌

## DURHAM

### DUN COW
37 Old Elvet, DH1 3HN

☼ 11 (10 Sat)-11; 12-10.30 Sun
☎ (0191) 386 9219

This marvellous, black-and-white timbered and creakingly ancient ale house dates from either the sixteenth or seventeenth centuries, opinion is divided, and the name is a corruption of Dunelm, the original name for Durham. The tiny front bar is opened by a sliding door and has panelled walls, built-in wall settles, a beamed ceiling with a collection of jugs, and a bricked-in fireplace. Of special interest is an old print showing cricket being played on a ground below the cathedral. The bigger back-bar is reached by a passageway that contains plaques outlining the history of the pub, the city and the legend of the local saint, Cuthbert, whose remains lie in the cathedral. Sport is shown on a screen in the back-bar, which has generous seating and a stove for cold days. The two regular beers in the Dun Cow are Caledonian Deuchars IPA and Cameron's Castle Eden Ale, supplemented by regular guest beers. The pub is the biggest outlet for Castle Eden in the country. Lunchtime food is served.

Q ❀ ◑ ⊞ ♣

### SHAKESPEARE
63 Saddler Street, DH1 3NU

☼ 11-11; 12-10.30 Sun
☎ (0191) 384 3261

The Shakespeare has no known connections with the Bard but it is always good to see England's great playwright commemorated. It is worth a quick glance at the exterior of the pub before sampling the joys inside, for the inn was once an example of 'Brewer's Tudor', all fake black and white timbers outside. The owners, Scottish & Newcastle, have sensitively turned it back into a genuine, early nineteenth-century tavern. The pub is on CAMRA's National Inventory of Pubs with historic interiors and if you step inside you will see why it deserves the accolade. The front lounge is tiny, dominated by its bar and wooden bench seats. A narrow passageway leads to a tiny snug and a second lounge. The snug was threatened with demolition in the 1990s and was saved as the result of a campaign by the local branch of CAMRA. The back rooms have wall settles and wooden floors, photos of actors from yesteryear, portraits of Durham in the 1930s and, fittingly, a collection of the complete works of Shakespeare. The inn serves Caledonian Deuchars IPA and McEwan's 80 Shilling and has guest beers such as Fuller's London Pride. The Shakespeare is well placed for visiting Durham market place and cathedral.

🐴 ♿ ⊞

## WOODMAN INN
23 Gilesgate, DH1 1QW

✪ 12-midnight; 12-11.30 Sun
☎ (0191) 386 7500

If the Shakespeare is tiny, the Woodman is a pub of a different colour. There's a comfortable front lounge with generous seating, a large serving area to the left and then a vast back room dominated by a pool table. The Woodman's main claim to fame is that it is a major outlet for the Durham Brewery based at Bowburn. The brewery is dedicated to all matters ecclesiastical in the area and its range of beers includes Bede's Gold, Prior's Gold, White Friar, Bishop's Gold, Cuthbert's Cross, White and Black Bishops, Evensong and Magnificat. On my visit, the Woodman was serving Bede's Gold, Fog on the Tyne from Northumberland, another North-east craft brewery, as well as the more familiar if far-flung Shepherd Neame Bitter from Kent. The pub stages regular beer festivals, including some with a German theme. Photographs on the walls point to the licensee's passion for Border terriers.

**Other Cricket Grounds**
*Durham CCC also plays at Darlington*

## DARLINGTON

### DARLINGTON CRICKET AND ATHLETIC CLUB
Feethams Cricket Ground
South Terrace, Darlington, Co Durham, DL1 5JD

☎ (01325) 250044 (including prospects for play)
✪ 7.30 (7 Fri; 12 Sat)-midnight; 12-11.30 Sun;
bar opens earlier when matches are played.

The pavilion at the club has a lounge decorated with local cricketing memorabilia. Members select the guest beers on a monthly basis. You will need to show a CAMRA membership card or a copy of the Good Beer Guide to gain entry.

**Beers:** Cameron's Strongarm and guest beers.

✿ ≈ ♣ P

### BRITANNIA
Archer Street, DL3 6LR
(next to ring road, west of town centre)

✪ 11.30-3, 5.30-11; 11.30-11 Fri & Sat;
12-10.30 Sun
☎ (01325) 463787

**Beers:** Cameron's Strongarm, John Smith's Bitter and guest beers.

⚲ Q ♿ ≈ ♣ P ⊟

*Binns Department Store, 1-7 High Row
(T (0870) 160 7273) has a renowned range of international beers in the basement, including Belgian beers and bottle-conditioned British ales.*

# ESSEX

### ESSEX COUNTY CRICKET CLUB
County Cricket Ground
New Writtle Street, Chelmsford, Essex, CM2 0PG

☎ (01245) 252420 for general enquiries
0871 871 6166 for prospects of play
www.essexcricket.org.uk
Email: administration.essex@ecb.co.uk

### Getting There
The ground is 10 minutes' walk from the railway station.
You can pick up a free map from the information shop at the
station and directions to the ground are well signposted.

Chelmsford is a delightful ground: small, intimate and friendly, with a
capacity of 6,000. The ground is well attended and supporters are
knowledgeable and generous to both home and visiting teams, but
major changes are planned: the ground is to close for a year in 2008
to enable redevelopment to take place. All home matches will be played
at Colchester and Southend-on-Sea for the duration of the 2008 season.
Chelmsford will reopen for the 2009 season and its fine collection of
memorabilia will move from the pavilion to a new museum. This will be
a great improvement: at present, only club members can view the artefacts, whereas the new museum will be open to the general public.

The Chelmsford ground is so bound up with the history of Essex CCC,
founded in 1876, that it comes as something of a shock to learn that it has
been the club's headquarters only since 1967. The ground was used inter-
mittently between the 1920s and the 1950s, when the club rented it, but in
those days the official headquarters were at Leyton, which is now in Greater
London. In 1964, the club raised the funds to buy the Chelmsford ground for
the peppercorn sum of £15,000: it is worth millions today. The ground is in
a fine location, close to the confluence of the rivers Can and Chelmer, and
with a large and attractive park to one side. A much greater sum,
£750,000, was spent on building the pavilion and other stands. In 2002,
the club was given permission to install permanent floodlights at the ground,
which allow day/night and Twenty20 games to be staged. Twenty20
games have proved to be extremely popular, with the ground full to capacity.
Chelmsford is too small to stage Test matches, as capacity is restricted by the
proximity of the River Can, but One Day Internationals are played there,
including two World Cup games in 1999. In 1998, Graham Gooch
scored 275 against Kent and in 2002 SS Das, India's opening batsman,

scored 250 in the tourists' match against the county, overhauling the 244 scored by Wally Hammond for Gloucestershire in 1928.

The pavilion's collection of memorabilia includes several old bats (one dating from 1870) and cricket balls, including the one used by Neil Foster and Norbert Phillip when they bowled out Surrey for 14 runs in 1983. There is a dinner menu for a celebration to mark Trevor Bailey's great career at the club and photos of club captains from 1876. Bailey, among other contributions, will be remembered for the slowest 50 in Test cricket – 68 runs in 357 minutes against Australia in Brisbane during the 1958-59 tour.

### Beer at the ground

The bar in the pavilion has handpumps for Shepherd Neame Master Brew Best Bitter and Spitfire: it is surprising at first glance to discover that 'Sheps' from Faversham in Kent sponsors Essex, but the brewery has a long association with the county and during World War Two was given a special dispensation to supply beer to areas of Essex close the Thames and the crossing to Kent.

---

### GREAT FEATS

☆ Graham Gooch twice took part, with Paul Prichard, in the highest partnerships for the county: 403 against Leicestershire in 1990 and 316 against Kent in 1994. In the match against Leicestershire, Essex compiled an innings total of 761 for 6 declared. In sharp contrast, Essex were twice bowled out for 65 by Worcestershire in 1947 and 1973.

☆ The lowest innings against the county was the already mentioned 14 by Surrey in 1983.

☆ The county's highest individual innings was 275 by Graham Gooch against Kent in 1988.

☆ MS Nichols holds the best bowling performance for the county: 9 for 59 against Hampshire in 1927.

---

*Top left, Trevor Bailey, shown here demonstrating a stroke for younger members of the Essex County Cricket Club*
*Bottom left, Graham Gooch OBE, the most prolific scorer of runs in top-class cricket.*

## Recommended Pubs
## CHELMSFORD

## CRICKETERS
143 Moulsham Street, CM2 0JT

✿ 11-11; 12-10.30 Sun
☎ (01245) 261157

In common with many pubs in the area, the Cricketers claims to be a Gray & Sons house. But Grays stopped brewing in 1974 and was a pub company long before the rash of new 'pubcos' in the 1990s. Grays takes beers from Adnams, Greene King and Mighty Oak and allows it tenants to choose from a monthly list of guest beers. Moulsham Street is a short walk from the cricket ground and has many pubs: you will have to go to the far end to find the Cricketers. The front bar is spacious, with cushioned wall-seats and tables and chairs set on bare boards. Some of the walls have been rendered back to bare bricks. Cricketing memorabilia includes an Essex sweater from the mid-1990s and a signed print of Graham Gooch. An iron grill between the bar and the pool room has a bat and stumps motif and the smaller back bar is packed with cricketing prints and memorabilia plus a Whisky Trail map of Scotland. Not only is landlord Kevin Harley a keen Essex supporter he is also a long-standing Hammer and his sons are also West Ham United fans: two have season tickets. It is a fine pub in every sporting way and serves Greene King IPA and Abbot and guests from Mighty Oak. Lunchtime food is served from Sunday to Friday and there is a patio area for eating and drinking in good weather.

❀ ◗ ⌷ ♣

## QUEENS HEAD

30 Lower Anchor Street, CM2 0AS

☻ 12-11; 11-11.30 Fri & Sat; 12-11 Sun
☎ (01245) 265181
www.queensheadchelmsford.co.uk

The Queens puts paid to the belief that people don't go to the pub any more at lunchtime, remaining instead at their desks with a lettuce sandwich and a bottle of water. On a midweek lunchtime, the pub was bursting at the seams and I had to wait to find a seat. The pub is handy in every direction: some three minutes from the Cricketers, eight minutes from the railway station and even closer to the cricket ground. On important match days you may well find some celebrated players and commentators enjoying a jar at close of play. The Queens is owned by the Crouch Vale Brewery based in nearby South Woodham Ferrers: twice winner of the Champion Beer of Britain award in successive years, 2005 and 2006, for Brewers Gold. The pub, run by Mike Collins, has a large beer garden to the rear that leads into a spacious back room with ample seating and photographs of such major cricket grounds as Lord's, Edgbaston, Headingley, the Oval and Old Trafford on the walls. The front section of the pub is dominated by a large bar with eight handpumps serving Crouch Best and Brewers Gold

and six guest beers from craft and regional breweries: Mike always has a dark mild and a stout or porter on offer. This wood-panelled section has more cricketing memorabilia, including photographs of CB Fry and WG Grace, plus a large Mann Crossman & Paulin brewery mirror: Manns was a famous London brewery based in Whitechapel, bought and eventually closed by the awful Watneys: two members of the Mann family were professional cricketers. The Queens has personal cricket associations for me: the inn sign, showing a happy Queen Victoria on one side and a grumpy one on the other, was painted by John Simpson, a CAMRA stalwart from the early 1970s and artist, cartoonist and graphic designer with whom I played for the Railway Taverners cricket team for many years; while Ollie Graham and Colin Bocking, who run Crouch Vale, are also keen cricketers. Like me, they have hung up their boots, but Colin does splendid work in the county training aspiring young cricketers. Their friendly and comfortable pub serves lunch from Monday to Saturday and also on Sunday if there is a match on. Live jazz is featured monthly on the afternoon of the last Sunday and there is a beer festival every September. Not too surprisingly, the Queens has been voted local CAMRA pub of the year five times, the last in 2006. Not to be missed.

♨ Q ✿ ◖ ♿ ⇌ ♣ ♠ P

## ORIGINAL PLOUGH
28 Duke Street,
CM1 1HY

✪ 11-11 (midnight Thur & Sat); 11-11 Sun
☎ (01245) 250145

The Plough stands next door to Chelmsford railway station and is handy for a beer before or after a match. It's large and open plan with ample seating and is dominated by a wood-faced bar that faces the entrance then turns right and runs almost the entire length of the pub. The floors are bare boards and there are fireplaces, wooden tables and chairs and leather sofas. A patio at the back provides outdoor drinking space. The Plough has a good range of cask beers such as Adnams Bitter, Caledonian Deuchars IPA, Everards Tiger, Greene King IPA and Young's Waggledance. Guest beers are chalked on a board above the bar. Food is served at lunchtime and evening meals are available from Monday to Thursday until 8pm. There are occasional live rock and soul events. The landlord is a keen Rugby supporter and shows matches on a large screen but also features other important sporting events.

## SWAN
School Road, CM9 8JL (2 miles SE of B1022, between Tiptree and Maldon)

✪ 11-11; 12-10.30 Sun
☎ (01621) 892689

If you're in the area, make the trip to visit the Swan. This seventeenth-century, heavily beamed village pub has twice been voted CAMRA's National Pub of the Year and has a brilliant range of beer, including Adnams, Crouch Vale and Mighty Oak. It also serves proper cider and Belgian beers, and stages a beer festival in June. There is a large garden and walkers with muddy boots and dogs are welcome.

♨ Q ✿ ◑ ⊞ ♿ ♨ ♣ ● P

## Other Cricket Grounds
*Essex also plays at Colchester and Southend-on-Sea.*

### COLCHESTER

**COLCHESTER AND
EAST ESSEX
CRICKET CLUB**
Castle Park
Sportsway, off Catchpool Road
Colchester

☎ (01206) 769071
(including prospects of play)

**Bricklayers**
27 Bergholt Road, CO4 5AA
(near North railway station)

✪ 11-3; 5.30-11; 11-midnight Fri;
11-11 Sat; 12-3; 7-11 Sun
☎ (01206) 852008

**Beers:** Adnams Bitter, Explorer &
Broadside, Fuller's London Pride.

❀ ◖ ⊞ ⇌ (North) ♣ ♠ P

**Dragoon**
82 Butt Road, CO3 3DA

✪ 11-midnight (1am Fri & Sat)
☎ (01206) 573464

**Beers:** Adnams Bitter, Explorer &
Broadside, guest beers.

OLGT (Town)

**Fox & Fiddler**
1 St John's Street, CO2 7AA

✪ 11-11 (midnight Fri & Sat);
12-10.30 Sun
☎ (01206) 560520

**Beers:** Mighty Oak English Oak
and guest beers.

❀ ◖ ⇌ (Town)

---

### SOUTHEND-ON-SEA

Garon Park
Southend-on-Sea, Essex, SS2 5FA

☎ (01702) 613000

This is a new ground, opened in
2005. Essex had played at
Southchurch Park since 1906 and
in recent times restricted the use of
the ground for a cricket festival in
July. But in 2005 the festival was
moved to Garon Park, which will
be developed as a Centre of

Cricketing Excellence to encourage
coaching for schoolchildren and
club cricketers.

**Cork & Cheese**
10 Talza Way, Victoria Plaza
SS2 5BG

✪ 11-11; closed Sun
☎ (01702) 616914
www.corkandcheese.co.uk

**Beers:** Draught Bass, Nethergate
IPA and guest beers.

❀ ◖ ⇌ (Victoria/ Central) ◗

---

### WESTCLIFF-ON-SEA

**Cricketers**
228 London Road, SS0 7JG

✪ 11-1am (2am Fri & Sat);
11-1am Sun
☎ (01702) 343168

**Beers:** Fuller's London Pride,
Greene King IPA and Abbot and
guest beers.

Q ◖ ◗ ♿ ⇌ P

*Lancashire's Dominic Cork celebrates taking the wicket of Essex's Ronnie Irani during a NatWest Pro40 League Division One match in 2006.*

# GLAMORGAN

## GLAMORGAN COUNTY CRICKET CLUB
Sophia Gardens, Cardiff, CF11 9XR

☎ (029) 2040 9380 (including prospects of play)
www.glamorgancricket.com
Email: info@glamorgan.cricket.co.uk

### Getting There
It's a pleasant 10-15 minute walk from Cardiff Central railway station to Sophia Gardens. Alternatively, buses 21, 25, 32, 33, 62, 62C and 65C from the station pass close to the ground.

Beer and cricket are closely entwined in Cardiff. The city is home to the brewing dynasty of Brains, whose brewery stands just a few yards from the central railway station. The company has long been a benefactor of the club, members of the family have played for Glamorgan, and William Brain – albeit playing for Gloucestershire –is famous for taking a hat trick of stumpings while keeping wicket in 1893. Brains commemorates this achievement with a special seasonal beer called Hat Trick and is the current main sponsor of the county club.

Glamorgan Cricket Club was founded in 1888 but the club had to wait until 1995 to have a permanent home, even though it became a first-class county as long ago as 1921. The club led a peripatetic existence, playing on many grounds throughout Wales. In 1995 it acquired a long lease at Sophia Gardens from the previous leaseholders, the Cardiff Athletic Club. Glamorgan had played here occasionally but most matches were staged at Cardiff Arms Park, which takes its name from an old coaching inn, the Cardiff Arms, which stood on the spot. When the Arms Park area was designated for redevelopment in the 1960s, a new wicket for cricket was laid on the former Gala Fields area of Sophia Gardens, a large recreation park donated to the city by the Marquess of Bute and named in honour of his wife. The final county cricket match was staged at the Arms Park in 1966, which then became a ground used solely for Rugby Union and now forms part of a complex with the new Millennium Stadium.

Sophia Gardens, while close to the centre of Cardiff, stands in an attractive sylvan location. Initially a small ground, with just a few stands brought from the Arms Park, it has undergone such dramatic changes that it has been granted Test Match status and will stage its first Test in 2009 after a major redevelopment of the site. There will be a new pavilion, which will include a museum dedicated to the history of Glamorgan and cricket in Wales, administered by archivist and curator Andrew Hignell,

## GREAT FEATS

✴ The highest innings total for the county is 597 for 8 declared versus Durham in 1997, and the highest individual innings for Glamorgan is 233 by Hugh Morris against Warwickshire in 1997.

✴ Best bowling performance in an innings for the county is 8 for 63 by AW Allin against Sussex in 1976. The best bowling performance in a match for the county is 13 for 127 by Rodney Ontong against Notts in 1986.

✴ The highest wicket partnerships for the county are 425 by A Dale and Viv Richards against Middlesex in 1993; 284 by JP Maher and MJ Powell against Essex in 2001; and 252 by MP Maynard and DL Hemp against Northants in 2002.

*Accomplished sportsman Maurice Turnbull played cricket for England, and rugby and hockey for Wales.*

and a new grandstand and media centre. Capacity will almost double to 16,500. Work is due to begin on the redevelopment in November 2006 and will be completed by the spring of 2008. There will be additional games at Swansea during the 2007 season but matches, including Twenty20, will continue to be played at Sophia Gardens: floodlights for short versions of the game were installed in 2004.

The new pavilion will have a Wooller Suite named in honour of Wilfred Wooller (1912-97), captain and driving force of the club for many years. His commitment and achievements are also marked by the Memorial Gates erected in his honour. But other heroes of Glamorgan cricket are not forgotten and, among others, suites in the National Cricket Centre and Premier Members' Lounge are named after Tony Lewis and Alan Watkins. Watkins was the first Glamorgan player to score a Test century, while Tony Lewis CBE ranks with Wilf Wooller as a great tyro of Welsh cricket, captain of England and chairman of the MCC.

The fact that Welsh cricketers have played for and even captained England points to the somewhat anomalous position of Glamorgan as a Celtic outpost of the game. Yet the county can point to the fact that, despite its slender resources and lack of a fixed home for most of its life, it has won the County Championship three times. At last, in 2002, the country was given the recognition it deserved by staging a One Day International against England, which Wales won emphatically by eight wickets. It is hoped that this fixture will become a frequent or even regular one.

The history of the club is enshrined at present on the floors of the Cricket Centre but most of the memorabilia will move to the new museum that will be called the National Cricket Museum of Wales. It will stress that cricket is not an English import: a game called Bando was played centuries ago throughout the country, using a bat, ball and stump, and cricket proper has been played in Wales since at least the 1760s, though Andrew Hignell admits the modern game was boosted when sons of the gentry went to English public schools and played cricket there. The corridor that leads from the reception area to the indoor cricket school will have a Heritage

Hall of Fame to enthuse young players, with a time line tracing the club's history from 1921 to 1997, when Glamorgan last won the County Championship. With the exception of the material in members' restaurants, the artefacts can be viewed by spectators who have paid for admission to the ground. There is a substantial library of books collected by Andrew Hignell's predecessor, David Irving, and when the books move to the new museum there will be a facility for borrowing titles. A collection of porcelain includes tiny 'coffins' or kitbags. Bats are held in a cabinet built by Frank Clarke, a Glamorgan player who was also a cabinet maker. They include one from a 1933 Test against the West Indies, which featured Maurice Turnbull, the first Glamorgan cricketer to play for England. The cabinet also includes a stump from the game against Hampshire in 1948 when Glamorgan first won the County Championship: Wilf Wooller seized the stump as a great memento. Another prized bat has the signatures of every Australian tourist who played against the county between 1909 and 1956 and includes Don Bradman's signature.

Glamorgan holds the unique record of beating the Australians on back-to-back tours in 1964 and 1968. Both games were played at Swansea and the club is keen to stress the Swansea connection. The Extra Cover Lounge depicts the victories against the Australians at the St Helens ground and also has a press display of the famous occasion there in 1968 when Gary Sobers hit the unfortunate Malcolm Nash for six sixes in an over. Press cuttings and a scoreboard mark the first County Championship crown in 1948. Photographs of former players include one of JH Brain, yet another cricketing member of the brewing family.

The floors and stairways of the cricket centre have further photographs of Glamorgan players from past and present. There is also a cap worn by Willie Jones, who scored two double centuries in 1948. Not only did he contribute enormously to the winning of the County Championship that year, but he also confused fielders of Essex and Kent while scoring his double tons, by calling to his fellow batsmen in Welsh. To stress that the Sophia Park area of Cardiff is proudly bi-lingual, all signs at the club are in both English and Welsh.

*Above, Wilf Wooller, batting against Middlesex at Lords in 1955.*

*Right, Wilf Wooller, captain and driving-force of the club for many years.*

*Below, Tony Lewis CBE, the first Glamorgan player to captain England in a Test match.*

## Y MOCHYN DU
Sophia Close, CF11 9HW

☎ 12-11 (midnight Fri & Sat); 12-10.30 Sun
☎ (029) 203 71599

The name means the Black Pig (there is a large painting of the beast in the restaurant area) and the attractive, half-timbered building was once the lodge to the park, with changing rooms available for players engaged in various sports. It is just a few yards from the cricket ground and the adjacent Welsh Institute of Sport. The main bar, with several intimate areas, pillars and comfortable cushioned wall seating, has a Cricketers' Corner with photographs of players and teams, and a bat signed by members of the Australian touring side in 1966. There are team shirts and a rather puzzling photograph of Ryan Giggs wearing a Welsh Rugby shirt: is he planning a late career move? A large screen TV shows cricket and other sports according to the season. The restaurant is sited in an attractive conservatory and the meals are highly recommended. Beers are mainly drawn from the Brain's range – Brain's Bitter, Reverend James and SA – with regular guest beers such as Cottage from Somerset. It's an attractive, welcoming and unusual pub, with bi-lingual signing.

❀ ◑ ◗

## CAYO ARMS
36 Cathedral Road, CF11 9LL

☎ 12-11; 12-10.30 Sun
☎ (029) 203 91910

This pub has everything for visitors to the cricket ground, which is just around the corner: good beer and food, accommodation (with a 10 per cent discount for CAMRA members), a meeting room and a fascinating history. The pub sign has a portrait of Julian 'Cayo' Evans, a horse breeder from Lampeter, who was a founder of the Free Wales Army. He instigated the setting off of bombs at the time of the Investiture of the Prince of Wales in 1969. Evans was jailed but died peacefully in 1995. In spite of my English accent, I was made extremely welcome and discussed cricket and football with the barman. The pub is open plan with polished wooden floors, a large curved bar, painted ochre walls and cushioned wall-seats. There's an impressive fireplace topped by a large mirror, and a framed shirt of the Welsh Dragons (the name of Glamorgan CCC in one-day or shorter competitions) signed by former captain Robert Croft. The Swansea-based Tomos Watkin Brewery supplies beers, including Brewery Bitter, Cwrw Haf and OSB, with a substantial input from Wolverhampton & Dudley – Banks's Bitter, Jennings Sneck Lifter and Marston's Pedigree. With such a brilliant range of beers and food served lunchtime and evening, this is an excellent 'tafern'.

Q ◑ ⊞ ⇌ (Central) ♣

Ilf you leave the Cayo and turn left you can glimpse the Westgate a few hundred yards away. This substantial building, designed with some Art Deco flourishes by the architect Percy Thomas, is just over the bridge from the River Taff and is handy for both Sophia Gardens and the Millennium Stadium: the separate entrance to Cardiff Arms Park is just a step away. The spacious interior is fronted by a large bar area, with tables and benches opposite, high moulded ceilings, the coats of arms of medieval barons as decoration, a lounge area to the left and a skittle alley. The walls have paintings of the old Brain's Brewery (it was based in the city centre before moving to the former Hancock's site close to the station) and a large painting of the founder SA Brain, who hails from Gloucestershire, not Cardiff, and which explains the presence of his descendent, William Brain, in the Gloucestershire team. The Westgate is a flagship Brain's pub and serves the full range including seasonal brews. The Westgate serves food all day: do try the Welsh mustard, it's red and uses honey.

## WESTGATE
49 Cowbridge Road East, CF11 9AD
*(junction with Lower Cathedral Street)*

✪ 12-11; 12-10.30 Sun
☎ (029) 203 03926

Q ❀ 🍖 ◖ ▶ P

---

**Other Cricket Grounds** *Glamorgan also plays in Colwyn Bay and Swansea.*

### COLWYN BAY

**COLWYN BAY CRICKET CLUB**
The Pavilion, Penrhyn Avenue,
Rhos-on-Sea, Colwyn Bay,
Clwyd, North Wales, LL28 4LR

☎ (01492) 544103 or
(01492) 545082
(including prospects of play)

**Pen-y-Bryn**
Pen-y-Bryn Road, LL29 6DD

✪ 11.30-11; 12-10.30 Sun
☎ (01492) 533360

**Beers:** Thwaites Original and
guest beers.
♔ Q ❀ ◖ ▶ ♿ ♣ P ▤

### SWANSEA

**SWANSEA CRICKET AND
FOOTBALL CLUB**
The Pavilion, St Helen's Cricket
Ground, Bryn Road, Swansea,
Glamorgan, SA2 0AR

☎ (01792) 424242
(including prospects of play)

**Brunswick**
3 Duke Street, SA1 4HS

✪ 11-11; 12-10.30 Sun
☎ (01792) 465676

**Beers:** Courage Best and guest
beers.
◖ ▶ ♣

**Eli Jenkins Ale House**
24 Oxford Street, SA1 4HS

✪ 10.30-11 (midnight Fri);
11-11 Sun
☎ (01792) 630961

**Beers:** Badger Tanglefoot, Brains
Bitter and guest beers.

◖ ▶ ♿

**Rhyddings Hotel**
Brynmill Avenue, SA2 0BT

✪ 11-11; 12-10.30 Sun
☎ (01792) 648885

**Beers:** Greene King Abbot, Webster's
Yorkshire Bitter and guest beers.

---

*\*Cardiff is an excellent drinking city, with 14 pubs appearing regularly in CAMRA's Good Beer Guide.*

## GLOUCESTERSHIRE

### GLOUCESTERSHIRE COUNTY CRICKET CLUB
Nevil Road, Bishopston, Bristol, BS7 9EJ

☎ (0117) 910 8000 for general enquiries
(0117) 910 8040 for prospects of play
www.gloscricket.co.uk
Email: enquiries.glos@ecb.co.uk

### Getting There
Bristol Temple Meads station is two and a half miles away from the ground, Bristol Parkway five miles and Montpelier station three-quarters of a mile away.
City Line buses 8, 9 and 78 from Temple Meads and 72 and 73 from Parkway pass close to the ground.

As you walk down Nevil Road, past surburban housing, it seems unlikely that a major cricket ground exists in the area. Suddenly, at the end of the road, you are confronted by the Grace Gates and beyond, offices and shops. Even now you are not prepared for the impressive size of the playing area and the attractive pavilions and stands until you move further in. Then it hits you: this is the ground that WG Grace designed at the end of the nineteenth century, one of his many remarkable contributions that helped transform the game towards the close of that century. Many first class grounds boast of their Grace connections, but Bristol was his home ground, built to Grace's specification. A plaque at the entrance shows him batting, with the simple inscription: 'To commemorate Dr WG Grace, The Great Cricketer'. The tablet was erected in 1948 to mark the centenary of his birth. The ground was previously an orphanage and it has changed considerably from the day in 1899 when Gloucestershire played their first match there against Lancashire. The club was founded in 1871 and played elsewhere in Bristol before moving to Nevil Road. Gloucestershire has had its fair share of financial troubles over the years. In 1916 it sold the ground to the Fry's chocolate company in an attempt to clear its debts. It bought the ground back in 1932, then sold it again in 1976 to the Phoenix Assurance Company. Again, the club bought the ground back and today it is run in association with the Royal & Sun Alliance group. The original nineteenth-century Grace Pavilion was refurbished in the 1990s, while the new Jessop Stand on the other side from the pavilion was built in 1999 for the Cricket World Cup, with the Diana Princess of Wales Education Centre below it.

Mike Simpson, the enthusiastic club archivist, has assembled some fascinating collections housed in the Grace Pavilion and the Jack Russell

*Right,
WG Grace
in 1874.*

*Below,
WG Grace played
in the first Test match
in England,
against Australia in
1880 at the Oval,
and scored the
first Test century by
an English batsman.
He died in 1915.*

Suite within it. The pavilion is open to members only, but the general public can have access during Twenty20 games and on other occasions can pay £3 to use the members' enclosure, where they can, and should, ask to see the museum. There are many photographs of the old team and of Grace in the pavilion, and paintings by Jack Russell in the suite named in his honour, while the upstairs Committee Room has a large collection of Wisdens.  In the room set aside for the museum, there is a Grace Corner, with a photograph of 'The Doctor's' grave in Elmer's End cemetery in Kent and another of the Grace family taken in 1867: the Graces once fielded a team made up entirely of family members. The scorecard of Grace's last match – Grove Park versus Eltham in 1914 – is on display, along with signed books and letters from the great man. Other artefacts include Eddie Barlow's blazer from when he coached the club between 1990 and 1991, a showcase devoted to the achievements of Wally Hammond, a collection of cigarette cards with photos of county cricketers, trophies, ties and old scorebooks. There is also a beer handpump that was the trophy awarded to the county for its success in the short-lived Brain's Challenge Cup in 1993. Gloucestershire has done well in the short form of the game: it is the most successful one-day side in the past ten years, winning seven trophies in five years. One Day Internationals have been staged at the ground since 1983, with matches played there during the 1999 World Cup and the NatWest competition. Floodlights have been installed to feature day/night and Twenty-20 games.

Across the ground, the Diana Princess of Wales Education Centre is named after the late princess, who was a patron of the club. The Centre is not open to the general public and is used mainly by schools: you would have to assemble a group of students if you wish to visit. There are talks on the history of the game, a collection of club trophies and photos of such famous players as Tom Graveney, Mike Procter, Jack Russell and Curtly Ambrose, along with drawings that show how the shape of the bat has developed over the years and how a cricket ball is made. Full-size models of Grace and current captain

## GREAT FEATS

★ Grace, of course, looms over all others with his amazing statistics: the longest continuous career in first-class cricket – 43 seasons from 1865 to 1908; the first cricketer to complete the 'double'; to score a hundred hundreds; to aggregate 50,000 runs and to take 2,500 wickets. He took 10 or more wickets in each of seven consecutive matches in 1874; and 12 times scored a century and took 10 or more wickets in the same match. Grace also scored 239 with the amazingly named SAP Kitcat against Sussex in 1896.

★ But we should not overlook the immense contribution made to the game by Wally Hammond, who had a better Test average than Grace's (58.45 to 32.29), scored 35 double centuries, and was the leading batsman in the averages for eight successive seasons. He topped 3,000 runs in a season three times. Hammond features three times in the highest wicket partnerships for Gloucestershire: 242 with BO Allen against Somerset in 1946; 226 with GM Emmett against Nottinghamshire in the same year; and 239 with AE Wilson against Lancashire in 1938. Hammond scored the highest innings for the county: 302 versus Glamorgan in 1934.

★ The highest individual innings total for the county is 643 for 5 declared against Nottinghamshire in 1946.

★ Best bowling performance for the county in an innings is 10 for 40 by EG Dennett against Essex in 1906 while the best bowling performance in a match is 17 for 106 by Tom Goddard against Kent in 1939.

★ Perhaps the most remarkable game ever played at Nevil Road was the one between the county and Australia in 1930, watched by a crowd of 15,000. Gloucestershire were dismissed for just 72 in their first innings but in their second innings Hammond scored 89, and helped the county to a total of 202. The Australian team, who included Don Bradman, made 157 in their first innings and in the second they were demolished by the bowling of Tom Goddard and Charlie Parker and were all out for 117. The result was a tie, which led to scenes of wild jubilation in Bristol.

*Left, Wally Hammond topped 3,000 runs in a season three times.*

*Below, Former Gloucestershire captain, Tom Graveney. His brother Ken and nephew David were also Gloucestershire captains.*

Mark Alleyne give a fascinating insight into how the kit worn by players has changed between the Victorian period and the present day.

### Beer at the ground

Marston's Pedigree on handpump is available at the ground for spectators as well as members.

**Recommended Pubs BRISTOL** *Bristol is great drinking territory: there are 29 pubs listed in the 2007 Good Beer Guide.*

## ANNEXE INN

Seymour Road, Bishopton, BS7 9HR

☼ 12-11; 11.30-11 Sat, 12-10.30 Sun
☎ (0117) 949 3931
www.the-annexe.co.uk

The Annexe is just three minutes' walk from the cricket ground and is part of a complex that includes the Sportsman pub and restaurant on the corner of Nevil Road and Seymour Road. The small, single-storey exterior of the Annexe doesn't prepare you for the spacious interior, with mock beams and settles, a pool room, and a conservatory and garden for families. TV screens show sport, while the walls are decorated with photographs of the Gloucestershire team and the season's fixture list. At first, the bar looks forbidding, with a phalanx of keg founts, but look beyond them to the cask beers and hand-pumps at the back. There is a splendid choice on offer: Badger Tanglefoot, Draught Bass, Courage Best, Sharp's Doom Bar, Shepherd Neame Spitfire and Wye Valley Bitter. Two further beers are added to the range to cope with the demand during Twenty20 matches. Food is served from noon to 7pm Monday to Saturday and 12 to 4pm on Sunday. Full restaurant meals are available in the Barn restaurant across the courtyard.

## WELLINGTON

Gloucester Road, Horfield, BS7 8UR

☼ 12-11 (midnight Fri & Sat); 12-11 Sun
☎ (0117) 951 3022

From the Annexe, walk back to the top of Nevil Road, turn right and walk for about ten minutes (the exercise will do you good) until you see the Wellington on the opposite side of the road, set well back and overlooking the wide open space of Horfield Common. The Wellington is a large red-brick building owned by the Bath Ales brewery, which is now based in East Bristol. It is spacious inside with a main bar area dominated by a black-painted servery, wooden floors and comfortable settles. There are smaller and more intimate areas leading off from the main room and a back garden where beer festivals are staged. The pub serves the full Bath range of SPA, Gem, Barnstormer and Wild Hare, plus many seasonal brews, and also offers the sublime Czech beer Budweiser Budvar in light and dark versions: try a pint of mixed. Food is served all day and I can vouch for the quality of the accommodation. There are regular live jazz and blues concerts on Sundays and Mondays. The pub was voted CAMRA's local pub of the year in 2004 and was joint winner in 2005.

The Inn, just a quick walk from the Wellington, was once a failing pub called the Royal George, serving keg beer. It has been revived thanks to a vigorous real ale policy and boasts a phalanx of handpumps for cask beer and a further six for proper West Country ciders. While the Wellington is all Victorian pomp, the Inn stands in sharp contrast as a thoroughly revamped modern pub, with a large open plan bar, maroon walls and barley white ceilings, settles and part wood, part flagstone floors. Beams are decorated with the pump clips of the vast number of beers sold in the pub, while a frieze of hops hangs from the ceiling. There is a comfortable lounge area to the left of the bar while to the right a former skittles alley has more seating, TV screens and a pool table. Food is available at both lunchtime and in the evening. The beer range is vast and changes regularly. You can catch the 75, 76, 77 and 585 buses outside the pub, which is handy for Bristol Rovers' Memorial Stadium.

## INN ON THE GREEN
2 Filton Road, Horfield, BS7 0PA

✸ 11-3, 6-11; 11-1 Sat; 12-11.30 Sun
☎ (0117) 952 1391

Q ✿ ◖ ◗ P

*Spectators soak up the atmosphere and the summer sunshine at Nevil Road.*

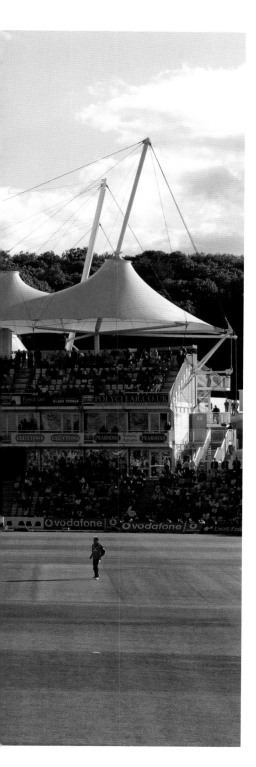

# HAMPSHIRE

## HAMPSHIRE CRICKET
The Rose Bowl
Botley Road, West End, Southampton, Hants, SO30 3XH

☎ (023) 8047 2002 for general enquiries
(023) 8047 2022 for prospects of play
www.rosebowlplc.com
Email: enquiries@rosebowlplc.com

### Getting There
The Rose Bowl is ten minutes by taxi from Southampton Airport Parkway station. Hedge End Station (Eastleigh-Portsmouth line via Fareham) is also 10 minutes by taxi. Both stations have shuttle buses to the cricket ground on certain days: check with the club.
Buses 29 and 29A run from the Airport Parkway Station to the Rose Bowl and Bus 8A runs from Southampton Central Station and city centre to and from the ground.
The cricket ground is also a short drive from Junction 7 of the M27.

You approach the Rose Bowl down Marshall Drive, named in memory of Malcolm Marshall and Roy Marshall, two West Indian players that made outstanding contributions to Hampshire. Ahead, you glimpse the canopies and raked spires of a cricket ground like no other in England, a cross between the London Dome and the cricket ground in Sharjah, with a touch of modern Lord's thrown in for good measure: the Rose Bowl was designed by the same architects behind the new Mound Stand. The Rose Bowl is, first and foremost, a magnificent ground for watching cricket, an amphitheatre with terraced seating that can be extended for major matches and the three-storey glass and steel pavilion with several hospitality areas, boxes and dining rooms. Behind the pavilion are rooms known as pods that provide space for offices, the media and scorers. The pavilion is curved to give an uninterrupted view of the cricket wherever you sit. Next to the pavilion are a cricket academy and a spacious and lofty Atrium Bar, which has facilities for the general public as well as members' dining rooms.

Hampshire County Cricket club was founded in 1863 and has had three previous grounds: it was based at the County Cricket Ground in Northlands Road from 1969 until the move to the Rose Bowl in 2001. The new ground was built alongside the M27 motorway on a site owned by Queen's College, Oxford, which it leased to the club in 1996. Money raised from the sale of Northlands Road plus a £7.2 million grant from the National Lottery were invested in the new site. The initial capacity was

6,000 but this has been increased to 9,000. The site also accommodates a health and fitness centre, squash courts and the County Golf Club. The first match at the Rose Bowl was played in May 2001 when the county played Essex in the Bensons & Hedges Cup, followed by a First Class match against Worcestershire. The ground was full to capacity that summer when Hampshire took on and resoundingly defeated the touring Australians. One Day Internationals are regularly played at the Rose Bowl and the first televised Twenty20 match was staged in 2003.

The Rose Bowl no longer answers to the illustrious name of Hampshire County Cricket Club. The development of the site required a total investment of £24 million and the club ran into financial difficulties. Rod Bransgrove, a local businessman, became chairman and raised the funds to finish the project. The ground is now owned by Rose Bowl plc and the club is called Hampshire Cricket.

On the ground floor of the Atrium, spectators can enjoy cooked meals and excellent beer. There is also a large display cabinet containing trophies won by the club. To the left of the main entrance is the Shackleton Suite, named in honour of the great Hampshire bowler: a montage in the bar is dedicated to his achievements, which include 2,857 First Class wickets at an average of 18.65. A further montage depicts Malcolm Marshall in action, while there are photos of players past and present and team photographs taken when the county won the Championship in 1961 and 1973.

The first floor of the Atrium has an honours board listing every Hampshire player since 1895 and paintings of past presidents and two long-serving captains, Lionel Tennyson (1919-1933) and Desmond Eagar (1946-1957). The Robin Smith Suite on the first floor has a striking montage of captains from 1946 to 2006, including Smith himself, John Crawley and Shane Warne. The club has more memorabilia from the Victorian period, including scorecards, old balls and bats that are currently stored in a portakabin and not on show at present: archivist Neil Jenkinson told me he hoped that the club would find room for a proper museum in either the Atrium or the pavilion. The

Shackleton and Smith Suites are open to members only, but in the close season or when no matches are being played it may be possible to view the rooms: contact the club in advance.

### Beer at the ground

The Atrium bar serves Courage Best and Directors along with Gale's HSB: the last named is now owned and brewed by Fuller's in London.

---

### GREAT FEATS

✴ The county's highest innings total is 437 against Surrey in 2001. The highest individual innings for the county is 166 by DA Kenway against Notts in 2001.

✴ Hampshire's highest wicket partnerships are 182 by Robin Smith and NC Johnson against the Australians in 2001, and 147 by DA Kenway and Robin Smith against Gloucestershire in 2001.

✴ The best bowling performance in an innings for the club is 8 for 90 by Alan Mullally against Warwickshire in 2001. The best bowling performance in a match for the county is 9 for 47 by AD Mascarenhas against Middlesex in 2001.

---

*Above, Former Hampshire player,*
*Lord Lionel Tennyson.*

*Above left, Hampshire's Alan Mullally ducks a bouncer from Australia's Glenn McGrath during the third day of the Fourth Test at Headingley, Leeds.*

*Above right, Hampshire's Malcolm Marshall pulls the ball to the boundary.*

*Left, The Rose Bowl ground looking towards the pavilion and main stand.*

## DUKE OF WELLINGTON
36 Bugle Street, SO14 2AH

☯ 11-11; 12-10.30 Sun
☎ (023) 8033 9222

Most of the city's past was destroyed by relentless bombing during World War Two, but there are still some historic buildings standing in the area by the waterfront known as The Quays, where you can also walk along what are left of the city walls. The Duke of Wellington is Grade II listed and is much older than the name suggests. It has been an inn since 1490, when it was called the Brewe House, while the cellar is even older, dating from 1210. It became the Duke in 1815. Once past the impressive half-timbered exterior you will find stone fireplaces at the either end of the main room, with wall settles, beamed ceilings, heavy wooden doors and a bar that seems to have been hewn from solid oak. Hops hang from the beams while military prints decorate the walls. The choice of beers is outstanding: Wadworth's 6X, JCB and Henry's, Ringwood Best, a rare sighting of John Smith's Magnet and Castle Rock Harvest Pale. Food is served from noon to 2.30pm and from 6 to 8.30pm Monday to Saturday, with a roast available on Sunday. A gem.

🏨 🐎 🕸 🍴 🍺 🍴 ♿

## PLATFORM TAVERN
Town Quay, SO14 2NY

☯ 12-11 (11.30 Thu, midnight Fri & Sat); 12-11 Sun
☎ (023) 8033 7232
www.platformtavern.com

This is another pub with a fascinating history, but one that has been given something of a modern makeover. The Platform, on the waterfront, was built in 1872 and takes its name from a platform constructed on the site to hold a gun battery and armoury to ward off attacks by the French, who had invaded the city in 1338. The spacious pub's main claim to fame is that a segment of the old city wall stands inside the main room. In other respects, the pub has an unusual modern décor, with African masks, statuettes and candles. The pub is famous in the area for its live blues and jazz concerts and prides itself on having no juke boxes or fruit machines. There is plenty of seating, including leather sofas where you can read the daily papers. To the right of the bar, a second room has more of a café ambience and is set aside for diners, though you can also eat in the main bar: good food is served at lunchtime, in the evening and all day Saturday, with a roast on Sunday. The pub's regular cask beers are Fuller's London Pride and Itchen Valley Godfathers. There are regular guest beers, too.

🍴 🍴

## Other Cricket Grounds

*Hampshire Second Eleven plays at the Rose Bowl and also in Basingstoke:*

---

### BASINGSTOKE

### BASINGSTOKE AND NORTH HANTS CRICKET CLUB

Bounty Road, Basingstoke, Hants, RG21 3DR

☎ (01256) 473646
www.basingstoke-sports-club.co.uk

**Basingstoke & North Hants Cricket Club**
*address as above*
✪ 12-3, 5-11; 12-11 Fri & Sat;
12-10.30 Sun
☎ (01256) 331646

The ground, known affectionately as 'May's Bounty', was founded by Colonel John May, owner of May's Brewery which closed in 1940. As well as Hants Seconds, the club is home to many other cricket clubs and has first-class training for young players, many of whom have graduated to Hants or Berkshire Minor County club. Pool and snooker can be played in the club and there are also squash courts. The club is members-only but is open to CAMRA members who must show a valid card.

**Beers:** Adnams Bitter, Fuller's Discovery and London Pride, Greene King IPA, Ringwood Best Bitter and guest beers.

🕭 ◖ ♣ P ☗

---

*And the crowd goes wild…*

*If you are staying in Hampshire, don't forget to visit the Bat and Ball at Hambledon, not far from both Portsmouth and Southampton.*

## KENT

### KENT COUNTY CRICKET CLUB
St Lawrence Cricket Ground
Old Dover Road, Canterbury, Kent, CT1 3NZ

☎ (01227) 456886 (including prospects of play)
www.kent-ccc.co.uk
Email: kent@ecb.co.uk

### Getting There
**Canterbury East railway station** is one mile from the ground and
**Canterbury West station** is one and a half miles away.
**East Kent buses** 15, 16 and 17 from the bus station to Folkestone pass
the ground as does the 399 from the city centre. Buses C1, C2 and C5
link the railway stations with bus station.

The Old Dover Road is a name that conjures up images of fog, the
rattle and jolt of horse-drawn carriages and the powerful drama of
Charles Dickens's A Tale of Two Cities. Today it is a pleasant suburban
road with one tremendous pub and is the base for one of the best-loved
grounds in the country, famous for the lime tree that stood within the
playing area and the highest individual score on the ground; 334 by,
guess who, WG Grace in 1876. Kent has produced some distinguished
players that have given great service to England, too, Colin Cowdrey
being the most celebrated. But perhaps the county's most singular
contribution has been its remarkable wicket keepers. In 1911, Fred Huish
took all ten wickets behind the stumps in an innings against Surrey at the
Oval and in his career totalled 1,253 dismissals, of which 352 were
stumpings. More recent 'custodians of the castle' have included Les Ames,
Godfrey Evans, Alan Knott and Geraint Jones, who have all played for
England. Huish and Ames are among the select dozen wicketkeepers that
have dismissed 100 batsmen in a season: Ames three times and Huish
twice. Ames also scored one hundred hundreds, reaching that milestone in
1950 during the annual Canterbury Festival Week.
    Kent, as befits a club based in the great hop growing area of
England, also has strong beery connections. Its main sponsor today is the
Faversham brewer Shepherd Neame, and Robert Neame, president of the
brewery, has also been president of Kent. In the nineteenth century, the
leading player Fuller Pilch of Norfolk was lured to Kent with the carrot of
running a tavern in Town Malling as well as playing cricket. When he
retired he ran the Saracen's Head in Canterbury. Another nineteenth-century player, Bill Bradley, was famous for his encyclopaedic knowledge of

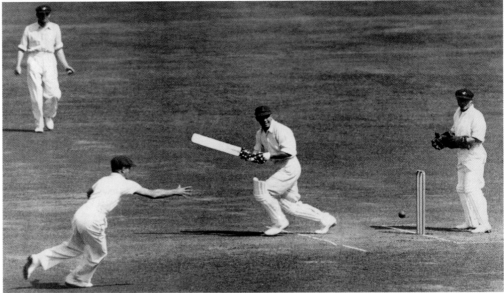

*Above, Kent and England player, Tich Freeman.*

*Right, Kent's Les Ames (second right) turns the ball to leg, watched by Yorkshire wicket keeper Arthur Wood.*

beer, while Percy Chapman worked in the brewing industry, Godfrey Evans ran a pub when he retired, and Rex Neame of Shepherd Neame played for Kent second eleven.

The county club was founded in 1847 and games at the St Lawrence Ground (named after a hospital that once stood on the site) were confined for many years to festival week in August. In common with Glamorgan, Kent led a peripatetic life, playing on nine grounds around the county. Today, Canterbury is the major venue, with 45 days of cricket every season. Tunbridge Wells is the only other ground to stage first-class county matches, while second eleven and limited overs, including Twenty20 games, are held at Beckenham.

Memorabilia is scattered around the Canterbury ground but it will eventually be housed under one roof when a museum and on-site hotel are built. One notable piece of history, the lime tree, is no longer to be seen: it was blown down in a gale on 13 January 2005 after a life spanning at least 180 years. As proof of its nostalgic pulling power, pieces of the tree have been offered for sale on ebay. A new tree has

been planted close to the site of the old one and, depending where the wicket is pitched, will be on the playing area. Only thee batsman – Learie Constantine (1928), Carl Hooper (1992) and Jim Smith (1939) – claimed to have cleared the original tree. In the manner of the 'lamppost cricket' played in the street during my childhood, players could be given out 'caught off the tree' but that rule was changed in the 1920s.

The dedicated and enthusiastic club historian is David Robertson who conducts tours of the main Chiesman Pavilion and other areas on certain match days and outside the season. The main pavilion has photographs of every capped player who has played for Kent, signed portraits of captains, a collection of bats and blazers, and a cabinet dedicated to Colin Cowdrey, containing his bats, blazers, caps and boots. A further collection of bats includes one from the 1790s and the bat used by Les Ames when he scored his one hundredth century. Some ancient cricket balls include one used by Tich Freeman when he took his 300th wicket in a season. Alfred Percy Freeman (1888-1965) was nicknamed Tich as a result of his lack of height (62 inches/157cms) and he was a master of leg spin and the googly. A scorebook records Grace's innings of 334 while a further cabinet is devoted to the achievements of Percy Chapman (1900-1961), who captained England when the Ashes were won and retained. He captained his country in seven consecutive Test victories, a record that stood until Michael Vaughan's side passed it. Chapman played four times for England on an Ashes tour before he had played a county game for Kent.

There is further memorabilia in the Cowdrey Stand, including the ball used by Doug Wright when he took his 200th wicket, and a heavily damaged ball, the result of an innings of 236 in 1924 by John Lindsay Bryan against Hampshire. This pavilion has restaurant facilities that can be used by members of the general public as well as members.

**Beer at the ground**

One of the major attractions of Festival Week is the celebrated beer tent organised by the local branch of CAMRA. This offers around 30 beers from small Kent-based craft breweries and from further afield, and such is the clamour that the tent serves some ten firkins (nine-gallon casks) a day. The event was started to raise money to support players' benefit years and is now also in aid of three charities. It is open to members of Kent CCC and their guests, but CAMRA members, naturally, are also welcome. The branch also organises a separate Canterbury beer festival in July. The pavilion bar serves Shepherd Neame cask beers.

For details of dates and times of beer festivals see:
**www**.camra-canterbury.org.uk
**Email**: gill@keay.fsnet.co.uk

*Above, Matthew Walker, shown here batting against Notts at Trent Bridge, holds the record for the highest individual innings for Kent.*

---

### GREAT FEATS

☆ Pride of place must go to WG Grace for his monumental 344 for MCC against the county in 1876.

☆ The highest innings total for Kent is 616 for 7 declared against Somerset in 1996, while the highest innings total against the county is 676 by the Australians in 1921. The lowest innings total against the county was just 37 by the Philadelphians in 1908 (is that why the Americans gave up cricket?). The highest individual innings for Kent is 275 by Matthew Walker against Somerset in 1996.

☆ Highest wicket partnerships for Kent are 366 by SG Hinks and NR Taylor against Middlesex in 1990 and 300 by NR Taylor and MR Benson against Derbyshire in 1991. Best bowling performance for Kent is 9 for 35 by J Jackson against England in 1858.

☆ The best bowling performance in a match for the county is 15 for 94 by Tich Freeman against Somerset in 1931 while the best bowling performance in a match against the county is 15 for 147 by WG Grace for MCC in 1873.

☆ The biggest crowd occurred when 23,000 people turned out to watch the Australians in 1948.

## PHOENIX
67 Old Dover Road, CT1 3DB

🕐 11-11; 12-4; 7-10.30 Sun
☎ (01227) 464220
**www.**thephoenix-canterbury.co.uk

Opposite the main entrance to the ground is the aptly named Bat & Ball. The pub has engraved windows promoting the long defunct George Beer & Co's Pale Ales. For a cornucopia of beery delights, however, I would recommend walking the short distance down the hill to the Phoenix where the landlords have built a reputation for running the finest outlet for cask beer in the city. The Phoenix has been named CAMRA Pub of the Year more times than you can shake a cricket stump at. The Phoenix has a spacious open-plan main room with a wood-panelled bar topped by a frieze of hops. The ceiling and walls are decorated with beer mats and pump clips. An engraved mirror of Canterbury Cathedral hangs above the central fireplace and, in the Gents, there's a mural of an umpire and three stumps. There are photographs of cricketers past and present in the bar. Greene King Abbot, Wells Bombardier and Young's Bitter are regulars and the guest beers are drawn from smaller brewers and may include Deuchar's IPA, Everard's Sunchaser or Milestone Black Pearl as well as a dark stout or mild. Food is available at lunchtime and in the evening (not on Thursdays) and bed and breakfast accommodation is on hand.

🏚 Q ❀ 🛏 🍺 🍺 ♿ 🚆 (East) ♣ P

## KING'S HEAD
24 Wincheap, CT1 3RY

🕐 12-2.30; 4.45-midnight; 12-midnight Sat; 12-11.30 Sun
☎ (01227) 462885

This striking fifteenth-century timber framed pub is Grade II listed and has a warm and welcoming interior with half-wood panelled walls, jugs hanging from the beamed ceiling, a collection of bric-a-brac and horse tackle decorating the walls. There's a frieze of hops above the bar and a collection of foreign beer bottles behind it. Bar billiards, a fabulous and under-rated pub game, is played inside, along with darts, while bat and trap, a possible forerunner of cricket, is played in summer in the attractive garden. The pub has Fuller's London Pride and Greene King IPA as regular beers but there is always a guest ale from a smaller craft brewery, such as Conwy's Castle Bitter/Cwrw Castell. Good value food is served at lunchtime and in the evening until 9pm (6.45 on Tuesday) and there is a separate dining room. I can vouch for the quality of the accommodation, as I stayed here. At night, the walk from Wincheap into the city centre is memorable, as it takes you past the floodlit cathedral.

Q 🛏 🍺 🍺 🚆 (East) ♣ P

## UNICORN INN
61 St Dunstan's Street, CT2 8BS

✪ 11-11 (midnight Fri and Sat); 11-11 Sun
☎ (01227) 463187
www.unicorninn.com

This atmospheric inn dates from 1593, when a local woollen draper built it as a private dwelling. It became an inn in 1661. In the nineteenth century it acquired a reputation as a violent bawdy house, but peace returned at the end of the century when it became a tied house owned by the aforementioned George Beer & Co. In the twentieth century, Beer was bought out by Fremlins of Faversham. Fremlins had the great misfortune to fall into the clutches of Whitbread, which eventually closed the brewery. Today the Unicorn is run as a free house.
You are greeted by a cricket bat above the inside of the main door to stress the importance of the game to the city.
The centrepiece of the open plan room is a large horseshoe bar and an open fire is welcome on cold nights. Beers include Deuchars IPA and Shepherd Neame Master Brew, while there are often one or two beers from the Kentish Hopdaemon brewery. The pub is celebrated for its food, served at lunchtime and evening (not Sunday evening). Bar billiards makes a welcome appearance here too, and there is a pleasant garden. The pub is close to the historic Westgate and is handy for West railway station.

♙ ❀ ◖ ▶ ⇌ (West) ♣

## Other Cricket Grounds
*Kent CCC also plays in Beckenham and Tunbridge Wells.*

## BECKENHAM

### BECKENHAM COUNTY CRICKET GROUND
The Pavilion
Worsley Bridge Road, Beckenham, BR3 1RU

☎ (020) 8650 8444 (including prospects of play)

### Jolly Woodman
Chancery Lane, BR3 6NR

✪ 12-11; 12-10.30 Sun
☎ (020) 8663 1031

**Beers:** Adnams Bitter, Deuchars IPA, Fuller's London Pride, Harvey's Sussex Best Bitter and guest beers.

**Q** ❀ ◖

*\*Beckenham, as the telephone code indicates, is now officially in Greater London.*

## TUNBRIDGE WELLS

### TUNBRIDGE WELLS CRICKET CLUB
The Pavilion
Nevill Cricket Ground, Nevill Gate, Warwick Park
Tunbridge Wells, Kent, TN2 5ES

☎ (01892) 520846 (including prospects of play)

### Crystal Palace
69 Camden Road, TN1 2QI

✪ 11-11.30 (1am Fri & Sat); 11-11.30 Sun
☎ (01892) 548412

**Beers:** Harveys Sussex XX Mild. Best Bitter and seasonal beers.

❀ ♣

# LANCASHIRE

## LANCASHIRE COUNTY CRICKET CLUB
Old Trafford, Manchester, M16 0PX

☎ (0161) 282 4000 for general enquiries;
    0871 434 4000 for prospects of play
www.lccc.co.uk/www.lancashirecricket.net
Email: enquiries@lccc.co.uk

### Getting there
**MetroLink:** from Piccadilly Station or Piccadilly Gardens to Old Trafford (the stop serves both cricket ground and Manchester United's stadium).
**Buses:** 112, 113 and 720 from Piccadilly Station.
There is a hotel at the cricket ground, the Old Trafford Lodge (0161 874 3333; www.lccc.co.uk/lodge).

For all its grandeur, with its magnificent pavilion and the famous bell that announces the start of play and is surmounted by iron scrollwork with the red rose of Lancashire, Old Trafford is an approachable, down-to-earth place where you are quickly on first-name terms. Mention the current Lancashire and England player, Andrew Flintoff, and you get the response: 'Aye, Freddie'. You get the feeling there will soon be a Flintoff Stand, for the club commemorates its great players: there are already MacLaren, Statham and Washbrook stands to mark the great contributions made to county and country by Archie, Brian and Cyril of that ilk. Cricket writers are not forgotten either, with the Cardus Press Gallery named in honour of Sir Neville Cardus, the noble scribe of the game for many years on the Manchester Guardian. Fittingly, the gallery was opened by another Guardian writer and world-famous broadcaster, John Arlott, on the eve of the first Cornhill Test Match between England and Pakistan in June 1987.

Old Trafford can match the Oval and even Lord's for the Victorian splendour of its pavilion. The ground dates from 1864, replacing earlier grounds used by the forerunner to LCCC, the Manchester Cricket Club, founded in 1818. Lancashire played its first match in 1864 against Middlesex, while the first Test Match, England versus Australia, was held at the ground in 1884. The committee room in the pavilion has photos of former players and a collection of Wisdens. The Queen, patron of the club, is welcomed and given tea here. The Presidents' Room has photographs of the holders of this office since the 1930s, while boards in the pavilion list all the captains of both Manchester and Lancashire cricket clubs since 1818.

The centrepiece of the Long Room is a stained-glass window depicting two stalwart players of the nineteenth century, Richard Barlow and

*Right,
'Gentleman player',
Richard Barlow.*

*Below,
Eddie Paynter,
Lancashire
and England.*

Albert Hornby, supported by wicket-keeper Richard Billing. The club's curator, Keith Hayhurst, heard a rumour many years ago of the existence of the window in a private house in either Blackpool or Southport. Further investigation revealed a dark Victorian secret: Richard Barlow, a 'gentleman player', which meant he received no payment for playing, had a mistress who gave birth to his son. The stigma of illegitimacy was a terrible one at the time. Barlow had commissioned the stained-glass window with the money he made from his benefit year, but gave the window not to Old Trafford but to his mistress who in turn passed it to their son. Keith Hayhurst tracked the window down in the 1970s by repeatedly asking the question in the shops and hotels of Blackpool and Southport: 'Have you heard of a house with a cricket window?' When he finally found the house in Southport, he knew he was at the right place when an elderly man, who was 'the spitting image of Richard Barlow', confronted him. Barlow's son agreed to donate the window to LCCC and also handed over a priceless cap that Barlow had given to his mistress. In 1884, Barlow scored a century and then took ten wickets while playing for North of England against the touring Australians. William Murdoch, the Australian captain, handed his cap to Barlow at the end of the match and said: 'I raise my hat to you'. It was the first time the expression was used and it has passed into the English vernacular. The cap is in the club museum.

The library in the pavilion has photographs of all LCCC players who have also represented England, copies of Wisden and books about the club. The room is open to members and to journalists and writers researching either the club or cricket in general.

The museum, at the Warwick Road End, has been compiled with enormous dedication by Keith, a retired teacher and schools inspector with a lifetime's passion for the game. He is also the chairman of the Cricket Memorabilia Society. The museum is open to the public, not just members, on all match days and is free to visitors who have paid for admission to the ground. It has one of the finest collections outside of Lord's. The roots of cricket in the area are emphasised by a large painting of

## LAKER'S OLD TRAFFORD TRIUMPH

On 31 July 1956, Jim Laker took the final wicket in a Test Match against Australia at Old Trafford and returned the astonishing figures of 19 wickets for 90 runs. The only other Australian wicket to fall was taken by Laker's Surrey team mate, Tony Lock. The match was decided by superlative spin bowling on an uncovered pitch known in those days as a 'sticky dog', the result of heavy rain followed by hot sunshine. England bowled Australia out for 84 runs in the first innings, Laker taking nine for 37. England then compiled a massive total of 459. Australia replied with 205, England won by an innings and 170, and Laker took all 10 wickets in the second innings. Since that day, only one bowler, the Indian leg-spinner Anil Kumble, has taken all 10 wickets in a Test innings.

Neil Harvey, one of Australia's greatest batsmen, who in his time scored more runs than any Australian save for Don Bradman, described how Laker bowled him in the second innings: 'It pitched on or about leg and I thought I had it covered but it turned sharply and clipped the off bail. I have never faced a better ball than that.'

Two days of the Test had been lost to rain and there were only 6,000 spectators in the ground on the

Monday to witness Laker's triumph. When the last wicket fell – Maddocks LBW – there was no cheering or stamping by the crowd, just gentle applause and some claps on the back for Laker from members as he ran up the pavilion steps. As for Laker's fellow players, Tony Lock was angry that he had only taken one wicket and, as they left the field, only the Rev David Sheppard warmly applauded Laker. Captain Peter May, who also played for Surrey and with whom Laker had a poor relationship, turned his head away and said nothing.

Laker drove back to London after the match. There were no motorways at the time and, after a two-hour drive, he stopped in a pub in Lichfield off the A5 for a pint of beer and a sandwich. Customers were watching a report of the match on TV in black and white and nobody recognised the hero of the hour. It would all be rather different today: the crowd would have invaded the pitch, Laker would have been embraced by his fellow players, he would have gone on to make a fortune and would have been named BBC Grandstand's Sports Personality of the Year. In 1956, Jim Laker was paid £75 for appearing in the Test and Surrey deducted £15 each for the two county

matches he missed as a result of his England duty. (See 19-90: Jim Laker by Brian Scovell, Tempus Publishing, 2006.)

*Above, Laker takes the last wicket of the match.*

Manchester mill owners playing in the early eighteenth century. Cabinets contain trophies won both by Lancashire and by individual players. One cabinet is dedicated to Dr WG Grace, who seems, almost magically, to have connections with every club in the land:

members of his family lived in the Manchester area. The cabinet contains figurines of 'The Doctor', Toby jugs, a scorecard for a match in which one team was composed entirely of members of the Grace family, and the ball he hit when he scored his 100th century in 1895.

The collection includes an embroidered handkerchief presented to Eddie Paynter on his return from the infamous Bodyline series in Australia during 1932 and 1933. The handkerchief came from Paynter's Methodist church in Accrington and must have calmed him after the bitterness of the tour that was almost called off at one stage when the Australians objected to the ferocity of Douglas Jardine's tactics as England captain. On a more pleasant note, there are letters of thanks and admiration to Old Trafford from such luminaries as Richie Benaud, Don Bradman, Bill Edrich and Harold Larwood. The museum houses both the oldest cricket cap in existence, dating from 1875 and belonging to Vernon Royle who played for LCCC and appeared in one Test, a gold cigarette case presented to Ernest Tyldesley to mark his 100th century, and a curved bat from 1740. A more modern collection of bats includes those used by Grace, CB Fry, Archie MacLaren, Learie Constantine and King Edward VII. A large collection of cricket-related ceramics is said to be worth £10,000, although no price is

*Above, Current Lancashire batsman, Andrew (Freddie) Flintoff.*

*Right, rain stops play.*

placed on a pair of Brian Statham's boots, a more prosaic item. There is even a bottle of beer: a Bass Celebration Ale from 1982 that was brewed to mark the birth of a son to the Prince and Princess of Wales. The museum also has one stump from the wicket used at Old Trafford when Jim Laker took 19 wickets against the Australians in 1956.

### Beer at the ground

Cask beers supplied by Thwaites, including Lancaster Bomber, are available to members in the pavilion. Only nitro-keg or 'smooth-flow' versions are available for other spectators.

---

### GREAT FEATS

✳ The best bowling performance in a Test Match at Old Trafford is also one of the world's greatest ever performances: Jim Laker of Surrey and England took 19 wickets for 90 runs against Australia in 1956. The only other wicket was taken by Laker's Surrey team-mate, Tony Lock (see panel).
✳ Highest innings total for Lancashire in a first class county match was 676 for 7 against Hampshire in 1911.
✳ Best bowling performance was 10 for 55 by J Briggs against Worcestershire in 1900.
✳ Highest wicket partnership for the county was 350, scored by Washbrook and Place against Sussex in 1947.

---

### Recommended Pubs
### MANCHESTER

There are no recommended pubs in the vicinity of Old Trafford but relief is close at hand. If you catch the Metro back to central Manchester, you will spot the Briton's Protection on the right as you approach the G-Mex exhibition centre. Get off at St Peter's Square, scene of the 1819 Peterloo Massacre, walk back down Lower Mosley Street and past Barbirolli Square, and the pub faces you across the road. Barbirolli Square was so named in honour of Sir John Barbirolli, renowned conductor of the Hallé Orchestra. There is a bust of the great man outside Bridgewater Hall.

### BRITON'S PROTECTION
50 Great Bridgewater Street, M1 5LE

✪ 11-11; 12-10.30 Sun
☎ (0161) 236 5895

The pub, reputed to be a recruiting place for soldiers in the nineteenth century, is listed on CAMRA's National Inventory of pubs with interiors of outstanding historic interest. It has a long narrow bar, so narrow it is almost a corridor, with a tiled floor and wall settles. The bar runs almost the full length of the room and has an impressive bar-back with wine and spirits bottles. Look above you at the impressive gold-embossed ceiling. There are two smaller, cosy rooms beyond the main bar with etched glass windows and comfortable seating. The pub is owned by Punch Taverns, Britain's biggest 'pubco' (pub company) and focuses on beers from national or major regional breweries, such as Tetley Bitter, Robinson's Unicorn and Jennings Cumberland Ale, but there are always guest beers from smaller breweries, including Coach House from Warrington. 'The Brit' specialises in pies, including steak and Guinness, venison and wild boar. Food is available at lunchtime. The pub is handy for concerts in Bridgewater Hall but is on the move: as a result of local development, it will be transported – lock, stock and barrels – a few hundred yards away.

✿ ◖ ⊞ ⇌(Oxford Road) ⊖(G-Mex)

## PEVERIL OF THE PEAK
127 Great Bridgewater Street, M1 5JQ

✪ 12-3, 5-11; 12-11 Fri; 4-11 Sat; 7-10.30 Sun
☎ (0161) 236 6364

The Peveril of the Peak, named after a stagecoach in a novel by Sir Walter Scott, is just a short step from the Briton's Protection, though the step may become longer when the Brit has moved.   The wedge-shaped 'Pev' is also on CAMRA's National Inventory and has a magnificent yellow and green tiled exterior. The name 'Wilson's' above the pub sign refers to a long-dead Manchester brewery bought and closed by Watneys. Inside, the main room has a curved wooden bar with a striking gantry that has a stained glass motif. A corridor bar, a feature of northern pubs, is also served from the main bar. There is a traditional table football game and photographs on the walls show celebrities that have visited the Pev. These include Robbie Coltrane, Bruce Forsyth and the Gallagher brothers from Oasis. The Pev has long specialised in a good range of cask beers that may include Black Sheep Best Bitter, Caledonian Deuchars IPA, Copper Dragon Best Bitter and Wells Bombardier. Food is available at lunchtime and the pub opens early when Manchester United are playing at Old Trafford. The Pev was built in 1834 and has been run by the same family for 34 years: the current licensee is Theresa Swaninck, a Manchester legend.

**Q** ❀ ◖ ⇌ (Oxford Road) ⊖ (G-Mex) ♣

## OLD MONKEY
90-92 Portland Street, M1 4GX

✪ 11.30-11; 12-10.30 Sun.
☎ (0161) 228 6262

Joseph Holt is a Manchester institution, a fiercely traditional brewer of cask beer that will supply only its local trading area of 128 tied pubs. Holt's is renowned for the quality of its beers, including a memorable dark mild, and its remarkable prices: £1.45 for a pint of mild and five pence more for bitter in the Old Monkey. Prices are even lower in the suburbs. The Old Monkey opened in 1993 and was Holt's first foray into central Manchester. It is handy for Oxford Road, Piccadilly and Chinatown and has all the hallmarks of a traditional Holt's house: mahogany wood throughout, including the elaborately carved bar. There are leather-backed wall seats, and circular tables and chairs on the wooden floor. A sweeping staircase takes you to the dining room and bar on the first floor. Purely in the interests of research, I had a pint of mild, followed by a pint of bitter and then, in true Manchester style, the heavens opened and it rained heavily for an hour, keeping me prisoner in the pub. It's dark and lonely work, but someone has to do it…

◖ ⇌ ⊟ ⊟

**Other Cricket Grounds**
Lancashire also plays at Blackpool, Liverpool, Lytham and Southport.

## BLACKPOOL

**BLACKPOOL CRICKET CLUB**
Stanley Park, West Park Drive, Blackpool, FY3 9GQ

☎ (including prospects of play)
(01254) 393347

**Churchills**
83-85 Topping Street, FY1 3AY

✿ 10.30-11 (midnight Sat and Sun)
☎ (01253) 622036

**Beers:** Greene King Ruddles County and Old Speckled Hen; Marston's Pedigree; Wells Bombardier.
◖ ☙ ≈ (North) ♣

## LIVERPOOL

**LIVERPOOL CRICKET CLUB**
The Pavilion, Aigburth Road, Grassendale, Liverpool, L19 3QF

☎ (including prospects of play)
(0151) 427 2930

**Baltic Fleet**
33 Wapping, L1 8DQ

✿ 12-11; 12-10.30 Sun
☎ (0151) 709 3116

**Beers:** Wapping Bitter, Summer Ale, Stout; guest beers.
♨ Q ◖ ☙ (James St) ●

**Doctor Duncan's**
St John's House Lane, Queen Square, L1 1HF

✿ 11.30-11; 12-10.30 Sun
☎ (0151) 709 5100

**Beers:** Cains Mild, IPA, Bitter, FA, seasonal beers.
✿ ◖ ≈ (Lime St) ☙

**Brewery Tap**
(adjoining Cains Brewery)
35 Grafton Street, Toxteth, L8 5XJ

✿ 11-11; 12-10.30 Sun
☎ (0151) 709 2129

**Beers:** Cains Mild, IPA, Bitter, FA, seasonal beers.
✿ ◖ ● P

## LYTHAM

**LYTHAM CRICKET CLUB**
Lytham Cricket and Sports Club
The Pavilion, Church Road, Lytham, FY8 4DQ

☎ (including prospects of play)
(01253) 734137

**Hastings**
26 Hastings Place, FY8 2LZ

✿ 12-11; 12-10.30 Sun
☎ (01253) 732839

**Beers:** Black Sheep Best Bitter; Moorhouses Pride of Pendle and Pendle Witches Brew; Wadworth 6X and guest beers.
✿ ◖ ≈ ♣

**Tap**
Henry Street, FY8 5LE

✿ 11-11; 12-10.30 Sun
☎ (01253) 736226

**Beers:** Boddingtons Bitter; Greene King IPA and guest beers.
♨ Q ✿ ◖ ♿ ≈ ●

## SOUTHPORT

**SOUTHPORT AND BIRKDALE CRICKET CLUB**
The Pavilion, Trafalgar Road, Birkdale, Southport, PR8 2HF

☎ (including prospects of play)
(01704) 569951

**Barons Bar**
Scarisbrick Hotel, 239 Lord Street
PR8 1NZ

✿ 11-11; 12.10.30 Sun
☎ (01704) 543000

**Beers:** Moorhouses Pride of Pendle; Tetley Bitter and guest beers. Annual beer festival starts on May Day.
Q ☺ ✿ ⛃ ◖ ♿ ≈ ● P

**Berkeley Arms**
19 Queens Road, PR9 9HN

✿ 4-11 (12 Fri and Sat); 12-10.30 Sun
☎ (01704) 500811

**Beers:** Adnams Bitter; Banks's Bitter; Hawkshead Bitter; Marston's Pedigree; Moorhouses Black Cat and guest beers.
Q ☺ ✿ ⛃ ◖ ≈ ♣ P

*There are 37 pubs in Liverpool listed in the Good Beer Guide.

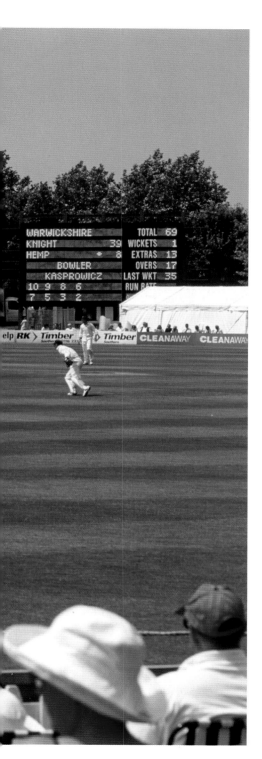

# LEICESTERSHIRE

## LEICESTERSHIRE COUNTY CRICKET CLUB
County Ground
Grace Road, Leicester, LE2 8AD

☎ (0116) 283 2128 (including prospects of play)
www. leicestershireccc.com
Email: enquiries@leicestershireccc.co.uk

### Getting There
**Leicester Midland railway station** is 2 miles from the ground.
**Midland Fox Buses** 26, 37, 37A, 47, 48, 48A, 68, 73 and 76 run
from Belvoir Street, a quarter mile from the railway station, to Aylestone
Road, then it's five minutes' walk to the ground. Alternatively, take
Corporation Bus 23 from the city centre to Aylestone Road.

There is a powerful beery connection at Leicestershire's County Ground:
the Cricketers pub (see below) used to be the entrance to the ground
and cricket can still be viewed there. The Cricketers stands on Grace Road
and surprisingly, for once, the thoroughfare is not named in honour of Dr
WG, but more prosaically, the daughter of a local house builder. Cricket has
a long history in Leicester. The game was first recorded in 1780 and from
that date many important matches were played at St Margaret's Pasture. In
1825 a new ground was built at Wharf Street, described as the finest
ground in England. Many representative matches were played there, including a few county games. In 1878 the Leicestershire Cricket Ground
Company bought 16 acres of land bordered by Grace and Milligan roads
from the Duke of Rutland. The first game took place at Grace Road that year
and in 1888 the county defeated the Australian tourists there. Leicestershire
became a First-Class county in 1895 and left Grace Road in 1901 for
Aylestone Road, which was slightly closer to the city centre. That ground was
badly damaged during World War Two and the county returned to Grace
Road 46 years after leaving it. Finally, in 1965, contracts were exchanged
between the club and Leicester Council and the sale of the ground, for
£24,000, was completed in January 1966. In spite of the address, and
though many famous cricketers, including Don Bradman, have played there,
WG never plied his trade at Grace Road.

While the ground has a modest capacity of 6,500, it is one of the
biggest playing areas in the world, measuring 147 yards by 167 yards,
second only in size to Melbourne. It has been developed since 1966,
with a new pavilion, and an indoor cricket school that also houses a media

centre and hospitality boxes. One-Day Internationals have been played there since 1983, World Cup games were staged in 1999 and the first floodlit match was held in the same year against Yorkshire. The Gower Suite next to the pavilion honours one of the club's greatest players of recent times.

The museum in the pavilion is open on all match days and has been painstakingly put together since the mid-1990s by the club's indefatigable archivist and historian Sylvia Michael. For my modest visit, Mrs Michael had gone to the trouble of producing ten sheets of printed information about the club, including the fascinating information that the first covers for pitches were invented at Leicester in 1926 by club secretary SC Packer (no relation to Kerry) who had earlier introduced Saturday play for the first time at any county ground. Mrs Michael also informed me that the drop in

the level of the ground from one end to the other is 18 inches and, before new drains were laid in the late 1990s, it could be underwater for days, with deck chairs floating across the temporary lake.

The Fox Bar in the pavilion (keg beer only) has photos of old players, trophies and medals. The main room has an exhibition that changes annually. On my visit it celebrated, with photographs and news cuttings, the contribution made to Leicestershire by Brian Davison, who played between 1970 and 1983, scored 18,537 runs and made 303 appearances; Ray Illingworth (who joined the club from Yorkshire), scored 5,341 runs and took 372 wickets for Leicestershire, and appeared in 61 Tests in his career, including 31 times as captain; and Charles Palmer CBE, who was club captain from 1950 to 1957, scored 12,587 runs for the club and took 291 wickets.

## GREAT FEATS

✱ The highest innings total for Leicestershire is 638 for 8 declared against Worcestershire in 1996. In 1956 the visiting Australians scored 694 for 6, of which Keith Miller scored 281. The highest individual innings for the county is 261 by PV Simmons against Northants in 1994.

✱ Leicestershire's highest wicket partnerships are: 390 by B Dudleston and JF Steele against Derbyshire in 1979; 320 by JJ Whitaker and A Habib versus Worcestershire in 1996; and 305 by JC Balderstone and BF Davison versus Notts in 1974.

✱ Best bowling performance in an innings for the county is 9 for 29 by J Cotton against the Indian tourists in 1967. The best bowling performance in a match for Leicestershire is 15 for 136 by A Woodcock versus Notts in 1894.

*Above,*
*Aftab Habib.*

*Far left,*
*Leicestershire's county ground has one of the biggest playing areas in the world; only Melbourne is larger.*

*Left,*
*David Gower, Leicestershire (left) and Graham Gooch, Essex (right) former stalwarts of the England Test team.*

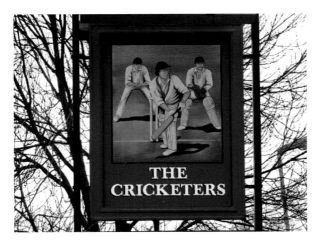

### CRICKETERS

1 Grace Road, LE2 8AD

🕑 11-11; 12-10.30 Sun
☎ (0116) 283 2026

1 Grace Road – could there be a more sought-after address for a pub called the Cricketers, even though, as explained above, there is no connection with the good doctor? The pub, once the entrance to the cricket ground, burnt down in the 1930s, was rebuilt and has been constantly upgraded by local family brewer Everards. By 2007, there will be a new family room extension, and a covered and heated garden area for those still addicted to the weed. The main bar is carpeted and has tables, chairs and settees while a second bar on the ground floor has a pool table. The windows in the main bar look directly on to the cricket ground but the best view comes from the balcony bar on the first floor, which has portraits of Leicestershire players past and present. There can scarcely be a better way to view cricket than from the balcony with a glass of Everard's Beacon, Tiger or a seasonal beer. The balcony bar can be booked for parties but is otherwise open to all. There are good simple lunches, too, with steak and kidney pie, fish and chips, three cheese pasta, vegetarian lasagne, chicken tikka masala and salads.

Q 🛏 ❀ 🍴 🍺 🕏 ♿ 🚌 P ⚓

### SWAN AND RUSHES

19 Infirmary Square, LE1 5WR

🕑 12-11; 12-10.30 Sun
☎ (0116) 233 9167

This wedge-shaped pub has become a Mecca for beer lovers in the East Midlands: it is a rolling beer festival, with two German festivals a year, regular real ale events and a cider and cheese festival on top. Not surprisingly, it was the local CAMRA pub of the year in 2001. The 1930s building has two bars with bare boards and comfortable tables and wall settles. Oakham JHB and Bishop's Farewell from Peterborough are regulars and the guest beers on my visit included Pegasus, a wonderfully chocolaty dark mild from the Milton Brewery, Mordue Workie Ticket and Radgie Gadgie from Newcastle, and Rugby 1823. The range of imported bottled beers is staggering in every sense: the golden Belgian ale Duvel, Orval and Rochefort from two Belgian Trappist breweries, and Gouden Carolus, a powerful ale from Mechelen. The pub also sells jenever or Dutch gin. Cheese and biscuits or filled cobs are available and Wednesday is curry night. The pub is handy for both the football and rugby grounds.

❀ 🍴 🍺 🚌 🍎 ♣

### LEICESTER GATEWAY

52 Gateway Street, LE2 7DP

✪ 11 (12 Sat)-11; 12-10.30 Sun
☎ (0116) 255 7319

The Gateway is just a short walk from the Swan & Rushes
and is in an area that was once the heart of the city's
hosiery industry but is now the base for one of the
faculties of De Montfort University. The pub is run by the
Tynemill pub company and is suitably sited in a former
hosiery factory. It's a large, open-plan pub with tiled
pillars, plenty of seating and a long bar with both handpumps for cask ale and founts for foreign beer. There are
always six cask beers on offer and the number rises to ten
at busy periods. These include Castle Rock Harvest Pale
and Everard's Tiger, with a rolling programme of guest
beers. Imported beers include Duvel, Chimay, Leffe and
Liefman's Framboise and Kriek from Belgium (the last two
are raspberry and cherry beers), with Budweiser Budvar
and Staropramen from the Czech Republic, and Erdinger
and Schneider wheat beers from Germany. The walls of
the pub have fascinating black and white photographs
of the hosiery trade. Food is available from 12 noon and
they offer a popular Sunday roast. The Gateway is a
good base for the football and rugby grounds but can
get busy on match days.

◖ ◗ 🚌 ♣ 🍎

*The Good Beer Guide lists ten Leicester pubs.

## Other Cricket Grounds

*Leicestershire also plays one or two matches a year
in Oakham*

### OAKHAM

### OAKHAM SHCOOL

The Pavilion
Doncaster Close, Station Road,
Oakham, Rutland, LE15 6DT

☎ (01572) 722487 (including prospects of play)

**Grainstore**
Station Approach, Rutland, LE15 6RE

✪ 11-11 (midnight Fri and Sat); 11-11 Sun
☎ (01572) 770065

**Beers:** Grainstore Rutland Panther, Cooking, Triple B,
Ten Fifty.

The pub is the brewery tap of Grainstore Brewery, based
in a former grainstore next to Oakham railway station.

Q ✿ ◗ ♿ ⇌ 🚌 P

## NORTHAMPTONSHIRE

### NORTHAMPTONSHIRE CRICKET CLUB
County Cricket Ground
Abington Avenue, Northampton, NN1 4NJ

☎ (01604) 514455 (including prospects of play)
www.nccc.co.uk
Email: post@nccc.co.uk

### Getting There
Northampton railway station is two miles away. Buses 1 and 51 from the station and 6, 8 and 15 from the town centre stop 100 yards from the ground

Northamptonshire, in common with Derbyshire, shared a ground for some years with a racecourse, in this case the Northampton Racecourse Ground in an area known as the Promenade. The first game staged there was a match in 1872 between the United North of England and the United South of England, which was won emphatically by the South by eight wickets. The county club was formed in 1878 and moved in 1886 to a new ground built on land in the Abington district of the town. A benefactor, Alfred Cockerill, guaranteed the club possession of the ground in perpetuity and in 1923 handed it to the club for a small rent for 1,000 years. The entire area is now owned by the club, though from 1897 to 1994 the ground was shared with Northampton Town football club. Football was played at one end of the ground and this restricted cricket when the seasons overlapped. When the football club moved to a new ground, cricket facilities were rapidly developed at Abington Avenue. The Ken Turner Stand was built in the 1950s to house the media, members' areas, and an umpires' room, while the Old Pavilion was refurbished in 1990 and 1991 and renamed the Spencer Pavilion: Earl Spencer is a keen supporter of the club. This pavilion includes a Long Room for members with photographs of players past and present. In 1979 a Players' Pavilion replaced the former Ladies' Pavilion: this has facilities for players, including a dining room and, on the ground floor, the Colin Milburn Bar, which commemorates the enormous contribution made to the club by the hard-hitting and larger-than-life cricketer who continued to play for a while even after losing an eye in a car accident in 1969. He was affectionately known as Ollie, as a result of a certain similarity to Oliver Hardy. He played for Durham when the club was a Minor County and he was

encouraged to move to Northants by the club
secretary, Ken Turner. He played only nine
Tests for England and was under-used by his country.
His greatest achievement came in 1966 when
he put Essex to the sword at Clacton, scoring 203
of the 293 runs in a match-winning stand with
Roger Prideaux. Ollie would no doubt have revelled
in the innings played at Northampton by Surrey's
Percy Fender in 1920, who scored his first century
in First-Class cricket in just 35 minutes. The bar
named in Milburn's honour includes some of his
county and England blazers and caps.

Since 1994, the old football stands have been
taken down and the main entrance to the ground
has been moved from the Wantage Road side
to Abington Avenue. This end now houses a new
and impressive indoor cricket school with a ground-
floor reception area and club shop. A hospitality
area, open to the public, has a trophy cabinet with
club ties, caps and balls. There are photographs of
teams from the 1930s, including one of Australia's
Keith Miller with a live kangaroo. There is a large
painting of Don Bradman on the stairs: the more
straight-laced Bradman eschews the company of a
marsupial. The ground is floodlit for day/night
matches and Twenty20 games, and it hosted
matches during the 1999 World Cup. The club
continues to develop cricketers of Test Match quality.
On my visit, as I entered the ground the first sight
to catch my eye was Monty Panesar wheeling away
in the nets. In the summer of 2006 he was taken
to the nation's heart just as Ollie Milburn was a
generation earlier.

### Beer at the ground

As Colin Milburn was known to enjoy a pint or
three, it is fitting that the ground has a bar named
after him. It sells Carlsberg beer – the brewery
is one of the club's sponsors – but there is often a
guest cask beer, such as Fuller's London Pride,
on handpump. The bar is open to the public on
match days.

### GREAT FEATS

★Northamptonshire's highest innings total is a
mighty 781 for 7 declared against Notts in 1995,
while the highest innings total against the county is
631 for 4 declared by Sussex in 1938. Scarcely a
great feat but it is worth noting that the lowest
innings total for the county is 15 against Yorkshire
in 1908, while the county bowled out Lancashire
for 33 in 1977. The highest individual innings is
329 not out by ME Hussey against Essex in 2001.
★Highest wicket partnerships for the county are
401 by MB Loye and D Ripley against Glamorgan
in 1998; and 375 by RA White and MJ Powell
against Gloucestershire in 2002.
★The best bowling performance in an innings for
the county is: 9 for 43 by GE Tribe against
Worcestershire in 1958. Best bowling performance
in a match is 15 for 31, also by GE Tribe, against
Yorkshire in 1958.

*Opposite page,
Colin Milburn batting
against Leicestershire
in 1963.*

*Above left, England
and Northamptonshire
player, Monty Panesar.*

*Above centre,
Colin (Ollie) Milburn
lost his left eye
in a car accident
that ended his
England career.*

*Above right,
Former Northampton
player Curtly Ambrose,
Wisden Cricketer of
the Year in 1992.*

*Left, Curtly Ambrose
in the final of the
1990 NatWest
Trophy against
Lancashire, at Lord's.*

## RACEHORSE
15 Abington Square, NN1 4AE

☣ 12-midnight daily
☎ (01604) 631997

It's a fitting pub to start with, given the racing origins of
the cricket club. The pub used to be on the old racecourse
which was closed when a woman spectator was killed
by a horse. It is a spacious, split-level pub with wood-
panelled walls dominated by a central bar. A railed area
to one side has photographs of Irish poets and play-
wrights and live bands play in a back room.
The Racehorse is owned by a pub group, Barracuda,
that gives the landlord considerable freedom in choosing
his beers. There are seven rotating cask beers, drawn
mainly from the Hampshire Brewery, but with contributions
from local brewers such as Frog Island, Potbelly and
Springhead. Budweiser Budvar lager from the Czech
Republic is also available on draught. Summer barbecues
are held in the large garden at the rear. Children are not
allowed in the pub but are welcome in the garden.

❀ 🚌 ♣ 🍎 P

## FISH INN
11 Fish Street, NN1 2AA

☣ 11-11; 12-10.30 Sun
☎ (01604) 234040

The Fish Inn is just off the town centre and close to a statue in the pedestrian precinct showing two children with a
cobbler's last: Northampton is still a shoe-making town
and the football team are nicknamed the Cobblers.
The pub has a striking exterior with a touch of French
château about it and internally is spacious and open-plan
with half-panelled walls, several raised areas, wooden
tables and chairs, and an enormous central bar with an
impressive back gantry that holds a collection of old
bottles. A large menu is available and there is a splendid
range of beers on offer, including the local Frog Island
Brewery's Best, Croak & Stagger and Natterjack, plus
Adnams Broadside, Courage Best and Theakston's Best
Bitter and Old Peculier. Frog Island is an area of the
town, not far from the railway station, that is often
flooded: hence the name of the brewery and the beers.

🛏 ◖ ⇌

## MALT SHOVEL TAVERN
121 Bridge Street, NN1 1QF

✿ 11.30-3; 5-11; 12-3; 7-10.30 Sun
☎ (01604) 234212

The Malt Shovel is a shrine to real ale. It stands opposite a building that is just the opposite: the Carlsberg beer factory. The factory is on the site of two former breweries, NBC (the Northampton Brewery Company) and Phipps. They were bought long ago by Watneys, knocked in to one and eventually sold to the Danish brewery. You will often find members of Carlsberg's staff in the Malt Shovel but I shall say no more on the subject in case Carlsberg calls in m'learned friends (and I will add in passing that the Carlsberg brewery in Copenhagen is beautiful and makes some splendid beers). The Malt Shovel is packed with brewery memorabilia, with many black and white prints of the Phipps site, and mirrors and plaques from other long-departed breweries, such as Benskins, Johnson & Darling, Lorimer, Mansfield, Mitchells & Butlers and Wards. The pub is one long room with a wood-panelled bar dominated by a phalanx of hand-pumps, while beer mugs hang from the heavily beamed ceiling. As many as eleven cask beers are available and the pub acts as the brewery tap for the Great Oakley Brewery in the village of the same name. Its beers include Wot's Occurring, Harpers, Gobble (named after a turkey) and Tailshaker. Other beers may include Frog Island, Fuller's and Tom Wood. Country wines and malt whiskies are also available, while live bands perform on Wednesday evenings and there is pub quiz once a month. The Malt Shovel was CAMRA Regional Pub of the Year in 2004 and is not to be missed.

Q ✿ ◖ ♿ ⇆ 🍎

# NOTTINGHAMSHIRE

## NOTTINGHAMSHIRE COUNTY CRICKET CLUB
Trent Bridge, Nottingham, NG2 6AG

☎ (0115) 982 3000 (including prospects of play)
www.trentbridge.co.uk
Email: administration.notts@ecb.co.uk

### Getting There
Nottingham Midland Railway Station/tram terminus is one mile away.
Buses 1, 1X, 2, 4, 6, 7, 7X, 8, 9, 10 and 11 link the station and
the cricket ground.
If you have time to spare, cross the road from the station and enjoy a beer
in the Vat & Fiddle, 12-14 Queen's Bridge Road, NG2 1NB, a Tynemill
pub that stands next to the Castle Rock Brewery.

Trent Bridge, the world's third oldest Test cricket ground after Lord's and
Calcutta, was built as the result of a pub and a cricket-mad bricklay-
er. In the 1830s, William Clarke, as well as laying bricks, organised the
Nottingham First Eleven cricket team. In 1837, he married a Mrs
Chapman, the landlady of the Trent Bridge Inn who also had the lease on
some open ground behind the pub. Clarke must have laid out a cricket
ground behind the pub with remarkable speed, for just one year later, in
1838, the first match was played there and in 1840 a county match was
played between Nottinghamshire and Sussex. The pub acted as the pavilion until a new one, at the opposite side of the ground, was built in
1886. In 1881, the cricket club signed a 99-year lease for the ground
and the inn. In 1919 the club bought both of them, though the pub was
eventually sold. The inn, known affectionately as the TBI, continues to oper-
ate while the William Clarke Stand commemorates the man who made
cricket possible at Trent Bridge. Clarke was a formidable slow underarm
bowler and also organised cricket matches throughout the country.

In 1899 an international match between England and Australia was
staged at Trent Bridge, while at the age of 50 WG Grace played his final
Test Match on the ground. Only Wilfred Rhodes played to a greater age
and he made his debut in the same match that saw Grace end his Test
career. Trent Bridge has also been a venue for football: both Nottingham
Forest and Notts County have played here before moving to their present
grounds either side of the River Trent. In common with Canterbury, Trent
Bridge had a famous tree, also blown down in a gale, this time in 1976.
The elm was known as Parr's Tree and was named after George Parr, who

*Right, Bill Voce, famous Notts pace bowler.*

*Below, Voce bowling against Surrey at the Oval in 1927.*

played for the county between 1845 and 1870, to mark the many occasions he hit balls into its branches. Miniature bats were made from the tree when it blew down.

I have always considered Trent Bridge to be the most attractive and convivial of major grounds and massive investment there in recent years has not spoilt its charms. On the contrary, the new Fox Road Stand, opened in 2002 by Ian Botham and costing £1.9 million, has replaced some rather tatty mobile seating installed for major games. The most recent upgrading has been at the Radcliffe Road end: the new Radcliffe Road Stand cost £7.2 million and includes the media centre, hospitality suites and indoor cricket school, as well as public seating. Boxes in the stand are named after famous Notts players and include Bolus, Broad, Hardstaff, Hemmings, Larwood, Rice, Robinson, Simpson and Voce.

The original pavilion, built in 1886, is the oldest in the country and is a treasure trove of memorabilia, lovingly assembled and cared for by the enthusiastic archivist, historian and writer Peter Wynne-Thomas, the author of The History of Cricket available from HM Stationery Office. He has built a library in the Squash Club Complex close to the Long Room that houses the second largest collection of cricket books in the world and can be inspected on request. The museum is in the members' area of the pavilion but is open to parties on non-match days: contact the club for further details. The Long Room has a collection of team photographs and the blazer worn by Bill Voce on the 'Bodyline Tour' of Australia in 1932/33. The museum has the largest collection of historic bats in the country, including one used by Derek Randall in the Centenary Test in 1977. Other collections include trophies and caps while the Long Room Bar has old cricket photographs going back to the eighteenth century and more bats above the bar, including those used by Grace, Jack Hobbs, Victor Trumper, Learie Constantine, CB Fry and Harold Larwood. Mr Wynne-Thomas, with his vast knowledge of cricket in the county, told me that 463 cricket grounds in Nottinghamshire have been or are still attached to pubs.

My memories of Trent Bridge are a mixture of good and bad. As well as some memorable games, I recall one Saturday of a Test Match when the weather was as cold as the depths of winter and the cricket so dull (Chris Tavaré was batting) that those of us sitting in the top tier at the old Radcliffe Road End turned round to watch a practice match at the Notts Forest ground across the road. On another Test Match Saturday, Richard Hadlee had Graham Gooch leg before for a duck in the opening over. The heavens then opened, play was washed out and my party retired to the Lincolnshire Poacher pub for the duration. Finally, during a One Day International, we had gone for a liquid lunch to a pub half a mile from the ground, over stayed the lunch interval and then heard a shout 'Botham's in'. Leaving our pints unfinished, we ran, staggered, panted and puffed back to our seats only to discover that Botham's stay at the wicket had been brief and he had been replaced by John Emburey. With great respect to the Middlesex tweaker, who would waste good beer to see him bat?

*Left, Nottinghamshire batsman Tim Robinson hits a four.*

*Below, Derek Randall batting against Warwickshire in 1991.*

## GREAT FEATS

☆ The highest innings total for Nottinghamshire is 739 for 7 declared against Leicestershire in 1903. The highest individual innings for the county is 296 by AO Jones against Gloucestershire in 1903.

☆ Highest wicket partnerships for the county are: 398 by W Gunn and A Shrewsbury against Sussex in 1890; 367 by W Gunn and JR Gunn against Leicestershire in 1903; and 345 by M Newell and Derek Randall against Derbyshire in 1988.

☆ Best bowling performance in an innings for Notts is 9 for 19 by J Grundy against Kent in 1864, while the best bowling performance in a match for the county is 17 for 89 by FCL Mathews against Northants in 1923.

☆ One of the most remarkable achievements at Trent Bridge was notched up by the Australian opening batsmen Geoff Marsh (138) and Mark Taylor (219) in the 1989 Test. At the close of play on the first day the scoreboard stood at 301 for 0.

## STRATFORD HAVEN

2 Stratford Road, off Bridgford Road, NG2 6BA

☼ 10.30-11 (midnight Thu to Sat); 12-11 Sun
☎ (0115) 982 5981

''The Strat' is based in a former pet shop and vets; its name was chosen as a result of a competition run by a local newspaper. It's a pun on Stratford-on-Avon and etched glass windows bear the image of William Shakespeare. The pub is part of the Tynemill group, founded by Chris Holmes, a former national chairman of the Campaign for Real Ale, whose pubs naturally have a powerful commitment to cask beer. Tynemill also owns the local Castle Rock Brewery and its beers feature in the pubs.

The Haven opens on to a small drinking area with a long, wood-panelled bar that leads into a spacious room. The walls are illustrated with cartoons, drinking memorabilia and brewery mirrors. A dozen or more handpumps serve such delights as Castle Rock Stratford Gold, Harvest Pale and Black Gold, along with Adnams Broadside, Bateman's XB, Caledonian Deuchar's IPA and Everard's Tiger plus a rotating programme of guest beers. Imported beers include Bitburger Pils from Germany and Liefman's Kriek. Food is served all day. Peter Wynne-Thomas, with his usual meticulousness, told me it was three minutes precisely from the pavilion end at Trent Bridge to 'the Strat' and he was spot on.

Q ♣ ◖ ◗ ⅃ ♿ ✤

## TEST MATCH

Gordon Square, NG2 5LP

☼ 10.30-11.30 (midnight Fri and Sat); 12-11.30 Sun
☎ (0115) 981 1481

In spite of the name, the Test Match is a good 10 minutes walk from the ground: after supping in the Stratford Haven, go back to the main road, turn right and keep going. It's worth the effort for this is one of the most remarkable pubs in the country and richly deserves its place on CAMRA's National Inventory of pubs with interiors of historic interest. As well as cricket, the Test Match is a shrine to Art Deco. Sitting in the main room, I felt I was floating on a luxury 1930s liner, a feeling underscored by a large painting of just such a boat from the 1930s. In the manner of the style, everything curves: wall brackets, massive central ceiling beams, even the ceiling itself. The windows are heavily draped, the floors are thickly carpeted and the walls are half-panelled. There are alcoves off the main room while the front bar emphasises the cricket connection with some magnificent murals depicting the game. Food is served at lunchtime and in the evening and is no-nonsense pub grub. The pub was owned by Hardys & Hansons of Kimberley in the outskirts of Nottingham and served Bitter, Olde Trip and Old Kim. In the summer of 2006, the brewery and its pubs were bought by Greene King and the beer range may change.

♣ ◖ ◗ ▣ ♿ 🚌 (6) ♣ P

## OLD TRIP TO JERUSALEM

1 Brewhouse Yard, NG1 6AD

☻ 10.30-11 (midnight Thu to Sat); 11-11 Sun
☎ (0115) 947 3171

This is England's oldest inn, carved from the sandstone rock below Nottingham Castle and another pub on CAMRA's National Inventory (see above). The date 1189AD decorates the whitewashed exterior and suggests the Trip was a meeting place for crusaders having a final glass of ale before leaving for the Holy Land. The only problem with this legend is that the word 'trip' did not exist in the English language until the fourteenth century and means a short journey or stagger, not a long hike to the Holy Land. The most likely explanation is that a brewhouse once stood on the site to supply ale to the castle and crusaders may have been given a farewell by the lord on the hill. The present inn is seventeenth or eighteenth century and developed out of that earlier ale house. Whatever the precise origins, this is a fascinating building, with caves open to the public, cramped but comfortable rooms on the ground floor, beer served from a hatch, and an upstairs cavern bar with its panelled walls disappearing into the dark of a rock funnel above. A more recent museum room houses a tapestry depicting Nottingham's history. Meals are served all day. The beers are Hardys & Hansons Mild, Bitter and Olde Trip, but under Greene King's ownership the range may change.

Q ❀ ◖❱ ⇌ ⊖ (Station St) ⊟ ♣

## Other Cricket Grounds

*Nottinghamshire CCC also plays at Cleethorpes.*

## CLEETHORPES

### CLEETHORPES CRICKET CLUB

Chichester Road, Cleethorpes,
Lincolnshire, DN35 0HZ

☎ (01472) 691271
(including prospects of play)

### No 2 Refreshment Room

Station Approach, DN35 8AX

☻ 9am-1am; 10-midnight Sun
☎ (07905) 375587

Beers: M&B Mild, Hancock's HB,
Hardys & Hansons Olde Trip.

❀ ⇌ ⊟

### Willy's

17 Highcliff Road, DN35 8RQ

☻ 11-11 (2am Fri & Sat); 11-11 Sun
☎ (01472) 602145

Beers: Bateman XB, Willy's Original.

❀ ◖❱ ⇌ ⊟ ⬤

*I'm sorry I can't recommend the Trent Bridge Inn,
which used to be a superb pub for visitors to the ground.
It has been turned into a 'youth venue' with loud music,
keg beer and lager. Sad.*

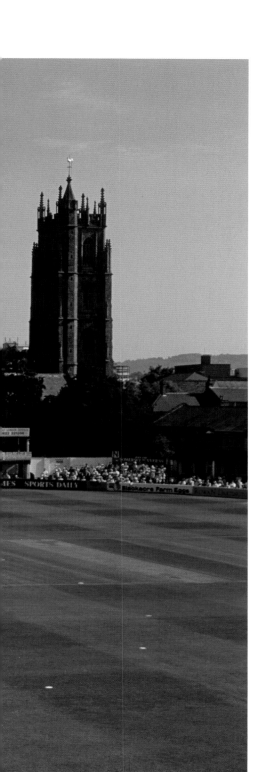

# SOMERSET

## SOMERSET COUNTY CRICKET CLUB
The County Ground
St James's Street, Taunton, Somerset, TA1 1JT

☎ (0845) 337 1875 (including prospects of play)
www.somersetcountycc.co.uk
Email: somerset@ecb.co.uk

### Getting There
Taunton railway station is a brisk, half-mile walk; the St James' Street end of the ground is closest to the station. There is also a shuttle bus service from the station to the town centre.

Somerset not only has a magnificent cricket museum but it is also housed in a superb building called the Priory, a barn that is the only remaining building of the Augustinian Priory of St Peter and St Paul, founded in 1158. The timbered barn, with an impressive vaulted roof, is listed and is separate to the county club. It is run by three volunteers – charming and helpful people – and is open Tuesday to Friday from 10.30 to 4pm, from April to the end of September. It is closed on Bank Holidays unless a match is in progress. Entrance is free to club members while general spectators must pay a nominal sum. Out of season, the museum can be viewed by special arrangement: telephone (01823) 275893 for details. It is located within the club ground and is accessed via the Priory Bridge entrance.

The two-storey museum has a series of well-lit cabinets on the ground floor housing a collection of caps belonging to such Somerset stars as Bill Alley, Ian Botham, Harold Gimblett and Vivian Richards, a pottery collection that includes a Toby jug of WG Grace, newspaper cuttings, Queen Victoria's walking stick, photographs of players past and present, Bill Alley's blazer, and a tribute to Gimblett, who scored 125 on his debut against Essex in 1935 and remains the club's greatest ever scorer of runs. There is a pictorial history of the ground, a collection of cricket balls and bats, including one used by Botham in an Ashes series: not surprisingly, it is badly damaged. Botham is the club's most capped player, appearing in 89 Tests while he was at Somerset. Another of the bats on display was signed by former Prime Minister Sir John Major. The most visually stunning artefact is a size 15 boot worn by Joel Garner. The upper storey is a library that includes a lending facility. There is a collection of Wisdens and The Cricketer, plus a large portrait of Don Bradman. With perhaps the exception of the Lord's museum, there can be no more impressive place to sit and look through records.

*Right, Somerset's Joel Garner also known as 'Big Bird' due to his six foot eight-inch frame.*

*Below, Ian Botham, one of the top English cricketers of the 1980s.*

The Somerset club was founded in 1875 and deliberately led a nomadic life, playing in all parts of the county until 1881 when the Taunton Athletic Club built a ground on Priory Fields, close to the River Tone. It became the cricket club's home ground and the lease was secured in 1885. The first match was played at Taunton in 1882 and Somerset was granted First-Class status in 1891, playing its first championship match that year against Lancashire. The Taunton ground vies with that of Worcester as having one of the finest views in the country, with St James's Church a few yards from the Priory Bridge Road end and the Quantock Hills beyond.

The ground has been sensitively developed over the years, starting with the Old Pavilion in 1891, followed by the River Stand in the 1950s and the Vice-Presidents' Stand in the 1980s. The Ondaatje Cricket Pavilion, with executive boxes and a shop was added in 1995 and a year later the Somerset Cricket School of Excellence was built behind it. The achievements of Ian Botham were marked in 1998 by the construction of a stand in his honour: this has boxes for the media and, given the reputation of the great man, what are quaintly referred to as 'refreshment facilities'. In 2002 the Priory Bridge Road entrance was given new gates and turnstiles and named the Sir Vivian Richards Gates. Richards is remembered for one of the most memorable innings at Taunton; 322 against Warwickshire in 1985. Graeme Hick of Worcestershire scored a massive 405 not out in 1988, while in earlier times Jack Hobbs scored his 126th and 127th centuries at the ground in 1925, overtaking WG Grace's record. Grace naturally left his mark at Taunton, scoring his 100th century here.

Taunton has staged One Day Internationals since 1983, including two games in the 1999 World Cup. More recently floodlights have enabled day/night games to be played. The ground has a capacity of 8,000 and while there are no trees to hit at Taunton, batsmen regularly hit the ball back over the bowler's head at the River End into the Tone.

## GREAT FEATS

⭐ The highest innings total for the county is 650 against Northants in 2001, while the highest innings total against the county is 801 by Lancashire in 1895. The lowest innings total for the county is 48 against Yorkshire in 1954 and the lowest innings total against the county is 37 by Gloucestershire in 1907. Viv Richards holds the record for the highest individual innings for the county: 322 against Warwickshire in 1985.

⭐ Somerset's highest wicket partnerships are 346 by LCH Palairet & HT Hewett against Yorkshire in 1892, 319 by Peter Roebuck and Martin Crowe against Leicestershire in 1984 and 310 by PW Denning and Ian Botham against Gloucestershire in 1980.

⭐ Best bowling performance in an innings for the county is 10 for 49 by EJ Tyler against Surrey in 1895. The best bowling performance in a match for the county is 15 for 95 also by EJ Tyler in the same match.

*Left,
Viv Richards, former
captain of the
West Indies team.*

### Beer at the Ground

The ground is a splendid venue for beer lovers: spectators, not just members, can enjoy handpumped Exmoor Ales, including Gold, Hart, Stag and Beast, as well as Marston's Pedigree. Moves by a 'major supplier' to have Exmoor's beers removed from the ground were fiercely resisted by the punters.

*Below,
Cricket memorabilia
at the Somerset
Cricket Museum.*

**Recommended Pubs**
**TAUNTON**

### COAL ORCHARD
30 Bridge Street, TA1 1TX

☀ 9am-midnight (1am Fri & Sat); 9am-midnight Sun
☎ (01823) 477330

This Wetherspoon's conversion is a shrine to Art Deco – a sort of Odeon cinema with beer. The low, false ceiling curves; there are curved pillars and round tables and both the long bar and the entrance doors have the three horizontal strips that are the hallmark of the Deco style. A bank of high stools behind plain glass windows allows drinkers to both enjoy a beer and watch the Taunton bit of the world go by. A room used for dining and by families is half wood-panelled and lit by fine Art Deco lamps. The main bar swells into another large area at the rear, also used by diners: an extensive menu operates all day. The pub stages regular beer festivals and offers a fine choice of cask beers on all occasions: on my visit Bateman's Strawberry Fields, Brain's Dark, Lees' Ruddy Glow, Marston's Pedigree, Mordue Five Bridge Bitter, Smiles Blond and Titanic Stout were available. Don't miss the amazing Art Deco toilets on the first floor.

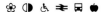

### EAGLE
46 South St, TA1 3AF

☀ 6-11.30 (midnight Fri); 7-midnight Sat; 7-11.30 Sun
☎ (01823) 275713

Please note that this pub does not open at lunchtime. Tucked away in a side street, this Victorian pub is a no-nonsense, traditional boozer that serves Otter Bitter from Devon, a splendidly hoppy offering, along with guest beers that often come from the West Country. The emphasis is on pub games, including two dartboards, two pool tables and two skittle alleys. There is an outdoor terrace for warm evenings that will no doubt be popular with smokers.

🎯 ❀ ♿ ⊟ ♣ P

## RING O' BELLS
16-17 St James Street, TA1 1JS

☉ 11-11 (closed Mon); 12-10.30 Sun
☎ (01823) 288574

This pub is just a few yards from the ground and stands in the shadow of St James' Church. The interior has been knocked through and, as well as pool tables, has a wealth of sporting memorabilia, including portraits of Bishen Bedi, Ian Botham, Joel Garner, Dennis Lillee, Clive Lloyd and Gary Sobers. There is a copy of the famous portrait of Nottinghamshire playing Lancashire at Canterbury in 1906. Changing sports, Bobby Moore holds aloft the 1966 World Cup in a fine picture while, somewhat incongruously, the bar also displays a flag of Derby County Football Club. Beers served include Courage Best and Sharp's Doom Bar.

🍀 ♿ ⇌ 🚌 ♨

### Other Cricket Grounds
*Somerset also plays at Bath (usually for one week in June).*

## BATH

### THE PAVILION
The Recreation Ground
Williams Street,
off Great Pulteney Street,
Bath, Somerset

☎ (01823) 272946
(including prospects of play)

### Star Inn
23 The Vineyards,
BA1 5NA

☉ 12-2.30, 5.30-midnight;
12-midnight Sat; 12-10.30 Sun
☎ (01225) 425072
www.star-inn-bath.co.uk

Pub dating from 1760 and on CAMRA's National Inventory. Owned by Abbey Ales.

**Beers:** Abbey Bellringer and Draught Bass with guest beers.

🏔 Q ⇌ (Spa) ♣

# SURREY

## SURREY COUNTY CRICKET CLUB

The Brit Oval
Kennington, London, SE11 5SS

☎ (020) 7582 6660 for general enquiries
www.surreycricket.com
Email: enquiries@surreycricket.com

### Getting there

The ground is only a few yards from Oval Underground Station on the
Northern Line. Vauxhall Railway Station and Vauxhall Underground
(Victoria Line) are approximately half a mile away. More than a dozen
buses serve the ground: contact London Transport Information:
(020) 7222 1234 or www.tfl.gov.uk.

Pubs played an important role in the formation of the Surrey club, now
based at one of the world's best-known and best-loved grounds. In
1844 the Montpelier Cricket Club played in Walworth on a ground owned
by the Bee Hive Inn. When the land was sold for housing in 1844, a member of the club suggested the possibility of creating a new ground at an area
known as Kennington Oval, which was owned by the Duchy of Cornwall
and was used as a market garden. The Duchy agreed to allow a cricket
ground to be built there and a lease for 31 years was signed: the Duchy still
owns the ground today. Things moved quickly: in March 1845 the splendidly named Mr Turtle (no slouch he) laid the turf obtained from Tooting
Common, and a match was played on it in May of that year.

In August 1845, the Montpelier Club convened a meeting at the
Horns Tavern in Kennington where representatives of more than 100 clubs
in the county voted, with wild cheering, to form one club for Surrey. The
inaugural meeting of Surrey CCC was held at the long demolished Horns
in October 1845 and the first Surrey match was held the following year
against Kent. The first County Championship game held at the ground was
against Sussex in 1873 and the first Test Match between England and
Australia was staged at the Oval in 1880: WG Grace scored 152 but
for once he was upstaged, with the Australian captain WL Murdoch
responding with 153 not out.

I arrived at the Oval in the spring of 2006 as the pitches were being
prepared for the season. I have watched more cricket at the Oval than any
other ground but it wasn't until I clambered up to historian Trevor Jones's
rooms in the pavilion that I appreciated the sheer size of the place. It has 27
pitches, more than any other ground in the world, and is exceeded in overall

*Above top,*
*The long demolished*
*Horns Tavern*
*which hosted the*
*inaugural meeting*
*of Surrey CCC.*

*Left,*
*Eric Bedser.*

*Above right,*
*Alec Bedser,*
*one of England's*
*finest medium-paced*
*bowlers*

size only by Melbourne. As a result, it has been used for other sports and entertainment: the FA Cup was staged at the Oval in 1872, 1874 and 1892, while a cup match between Australian Rules teams is held in the autumn. Cricket was suspended at the ground during World War Two when it was a German prisoner of war camp. (This may help explain why cricket has never taken off in Germany, save for Munich, where the MCC – Munich Cricket Club – plays, fittingly, in the English Garden. The club was founded by English journalist Graham Lees, who is also one of the founding fathers of CAMRA. and has an amendment to the laws that have not, I believe, been sanctioned by Lord's. The English Garden is surrounded by a track used in the summer by joggers who tend to dispense with their clothing. If a batsman is bowled, caught or in any way given out, he can appeal against the decision with the shout of 'nude jogger'. This means he was distracted by the sight of a jogger sans clothing, usually but not exclusively of the female persuasion.)

The Kennington ground, which is not a perfect oval – the shape comes from the surrounding streets – is today a mixture of old and new, where the world-famous gasholders still stand sentinel. The Bedser Stand and its accompanying Ken Barrington Cricket Centre were completed in the early 1990s and the names commemorate three of the club's legendary players, there being, of course, two Bedsers, Alec and Eric (Eric died in 2006). My father kept wicket for an RAF team during World War Two that included the Bedser twins. Further great players are marked by stands that have been renamed in their honour: Laker, Lock, Jardine, Fender, Gover and Surridge. The main entrance is named after one of the world's greatest-ever batsmen, Jack Hobbs. The most recent and dramatic development has been the overhaul and redesign of the Vauxhall End, seen around the world in all its modern cantilevered glory during the dramatic final Ashes Test in September 2005.

Amid all this upheaval, the Victorian pavilion remains as a magnificent monument to English cricket. The sweeping staircases have photos of every visiting national side, including one of an Australians team from the nineteenth century wearing long striped blazers that

# THE DON'S OVAL FAREWELL

Don Bradman, one of the greatest ever batsmen, made his last Test appearance at the Oval in 1948 for Australia. The enormous crowd stood and applauded him all the way from the pavilion to the wicket, where the England players gave him three cheers. He was then bowled for a duck by Eric Hollies: it must have been hard to bat in such emotional circumstances. Bradman's final Test average was 99.94. Eric Hollies said he didn't wash his hand for a week after getting 'the Don's' wicket. The Oval was also the stage for Len Hutton's monumental 364 against Australia in 1938.

In September 2005, England won the Ashes by defeating Australia 2-1 in the series. The final Test at the Oval was drawn. Can a draw be exciting? Yes, when the Ashes are at stake. England scored 373 and 353 and Australia replied with 367 and four for no wicket, when bad light stopped play on the last day. Kevin Pietersen scored his first Test century but the outstanding performance came from Shane Warne in his last Test in England. He took 6-124 in the second England innings and finished with a total of 12 wickets for the match. In total he took 1,000 International wickets in his career. Nobody who was at the Oval will forget the ovation he received when he came out to bat for the final time.

*Top right, Australia's Dan Bradman.*
*Above and above right, Jim Laker in action.*

make them look like convicts, which at the time could only have deepened the belief that all Aussies were descended from the 'criminals' sent – often, like the Tolpuddle Martyrs, on trumped-up charges - from London to Botany Bay. The pavilion also holds the famous obituary from the Sporting Times in 1882 when England lost a Test Match to Australia for the first time in this country:

'In Affectionate Remembrance of English Cricket which died at the Oval on 29th August 1882. Deeply lamented by a large circle of friends and acquaintances. RIP. NB The body will be cremated and the ashes taken to Australia'.

From that ironic paragraph, one of the world's greatest sporting contests evolved.

The Laker Room is dedicated to the exploits of Jim Laker, with blazers, scorecards and caps and, in particular, his feat of taking 19 wickets against the Australians at Old Trafford in 1956 (see Lancashire section). This room leads in to the Sandham Room, named after Andrew Sandham, who played for the county between 1911 and 1937. The Sandham Room contains a bust of Alec Bedser, memorabilia covering the career of Jack Hobbs, trophies, mounted balls, and a collection of bats, including a curved bat dating from 1729 and thought to be the oldest held in any collection. There is a prototype of the modern stump camera and a bat signed by all world leaders attending a conference in London in 1995 and organised by the then prime minister John Major, who is now the president of Surrey.

I have many memories of the Oval. They include rushing to the ground for the second day of an England versus West Indies Test, with Clive Lloyd unbeaten on a century over night, only to fall LBW first ball to Geoff Arnold; a stand of around 180 between Tom Graveney and John Murray in another Test against the West Indies;

*Left,*
*Old and new.*
*The Victorian Pavilion*
*(right), state of the*
*art OCS grandstand*
*(left) and world-*
*famous gasometers*
*(centre).*

*Right,*
*Mark Ramprakash,*
*2006 Player*
*of the Year.*

and the diminutive Alvin Kallicharran majestically hook-ing Dennis Lillee for six. I recall, as a child, the mirth that greeted the announcement that 'the next batsman is Crapp'. It would have helped if his first name of Jack had been used but professionals were addressed only by their surnames in those days.

Tours of the ground last for one and three quarter hours and cost less than £10. Further information is available from tjones@surreycricket.com and tours can be booked online.

## Beer at the Ground

Young's Bitter is available on handpump in the members' bar of the pavilion. There is no beer of any kind in the famous Cricketers pub that overlooks the ground and from where generations of drinkers enjoyed a free view of the ground from the pub balcony. It is boarded up and derelict.

### GREAT FEATS

✶ In September 2006, Mark Ramprakash was named Player of the Year: during the 2006 season he scored 2,278 runs at an average of 103.54.
✶ Highest innings total for Lancashire in a first class coun-ty match was 676 for 7 against Hampshire in 1911.
✶ The highest Surrey total was 811 against Somerset in 1899.
✶ Surrey's highest wicket partnerships were 448 by R Abel and TW Hayward against Yorkshire in 1899, and 428 by Jack Hobbs and Andrew Sandham against Oxford University in 1926.
✶ The best bowling performance for the county was 10 for 45 by T Richardson against Essex in 1894 and 15 for 83 by the same bowler against Warwickshire in 1898.

## Recommended Pubs
## CLAPHAM

*Kennington and the Oval are disaster areas for good pubs. It is worth going a few stops on the Northern Line for some excellent pubs in Clapham.*

### BREAD AND ROSES
68 Clapham Manor Street, SW4 6ED

☼ 12-11.30; 12-12.30 Fri & Sat; 11-11 Sun
☎ (020) 7498 1779
www.breadandrosespub.com

⊖ Clapham Common: walk down Clapham High Street and turn left in to Clapham Manor Street.

The Workers' Beer Company, set up by Battersea Trades Council, owns this fascinating pub. The company also runs beer tents at outside events, such as the Glastonbury music festival. The spacious pub carries a banner above the bar with the words 'Our lives shall not be sweated from birth until life closes; hearts starve as well as bodies; give us bread but give us roses'. The poetry was written during a strike by women textile workers in Massachusetts, USA, in 1912 and was later set to music. It remains a popular song at gatherings of women trade unionists. The upstairs function room has a series of paintings by a Canadian artist depicting trade union struggles. But you won't be beaten around the head with propaganda: it is first and foremost a cracking pub, with pale varnished wood floors, rosewood tables and chairs, and a large tan-coloured bar with a marble top that dispenses Adnams Explorer and Bitter, Battersea Bitter, Fuller's Discovery and Taylor's Landlord. A conservatory at the back can be used by families and is also the venue for regular beer festivals. There is a small beer garden at the rear and seats on a front patio. Excellent food includes soup, filled jacket potatoes, omelettes, Greek salad, sausage and mash, and grilled vegetable, mozzarella and tomato bake.

Q ⛵ ⊛ ◑ ◗ ♿ ⇌ 🚍 🍎 ⚲

**BREAD AND ROSES**

**MANOR ARMS**

**WINDMILL ON THE COMMON**

## MANOR ARMS

128 Clapham Manor Street, SW4 6ED

☸ 1-11.30; 4-11.30 Oct to Mar; 12-1am Fri & Sat; 12-11 Sun
☎ (020) 7622 2894

⊖ Clapham Common. Directions as for Bread & Roses.

The Manor Arms, or 'MA' as the blunt pub sign says, is just a few hundreds yards from Bread & Roses and offers a sharp contrast, one brightly decorated, the second more subdued and intimate. The Manor is a small, compact, single-roomed pub dominated by a horseshoe bar. The walls are half-pan-elled and there are comfortable leather wall settles and chessboard tables. The exterior is creeper-clad and there are plenty of seats at the front behind a fence and where children are welcome. Deep in the depths of south London, the pub has an almost rural air. A marquee at the back can be used by drinkers but children are not allowed in here. Sport is shown on two televisions in the bar. A fine range of beers includes Adnams Broadside, Black Sheep Best Bitter, Everard's Tiger and Taylor's Landlord. A good old-fashioned touch is provided by Clapham Manor Baths across the road, recalling a time when not all residential houses had bathrooms.

## WINDMILL ON THE COMMON

South Side, Clapham Common, SW4 9DE

☸ 11-11; 12-10.30 Sun
☎ (020) 8673 4578
www.windmillhotel.co.uk

⊖ Clapham South. Turn left outside station and walk down South Side until you reach the pub

Sumptuous sums up the Windmill, a large and superbly decorated pub, a good base if you are watching cricket at the Oval for more than one day, as 29 en suite rooms are available. I can't say with absolute certainty that the Windmill doubled as the Pontefract Arms in Graham Greene's The End of the Affair, but the main characters lived in the area and

regularly visited a pub on the common, so it was likely that Greene chose the Windmill. An inn has stood on the site since 1665 when the first alehouse keeper, Thomas Crenshaw, was also a miller with an adjacent windmill. The present pub-cum-hotel is Victorian and is built on the site of the home of the founder of Young's brewery in Wandsworth. It has several rooms, some wood-panelled, while the large restaurant area, which spills into a conservatory, has African artefacts blending with deep leather sofas. There are open fires, a domed ceiling in the restaurant and a collection of paintings by the artist Sonia Stait. The front bar has a good pub-style appeal, with wood floors, a moulded ceiling and plenty of tables and chairs, and is used by locals. There is a generous amount of seating at the front and in good weather customers also spill out on to the common. A wide variety of food is available. The beers are from the Young's range: Bitter, Special and Ramrod and seasonal brews.

🏨 Q ☕ ✿ 🛏 ◖ ◗ ⊟ ♿ ⊖ (Common/ South) P

**Other Cricket Grounds**
*Surrey also plays at Guildford.*

## GUILDFORD

### GUILDFORD CRICKET CLUB
The Pavilion
Woodbridge Road, GU1 1AJ

☎ (01483) 572181 (including prospects of play)

### Keystone
3 Portsmouth Road, GU2 4BL (on A3100)

☸ 12-11 (midnight Fri & Sat); 12-7 Sun
☎ (01483) 575089
www.thekeystone.co.uk

Beers: Black Sheep Best Bitter, Wadworth 6X and guest beers.

✿ ◖ ◗ ⇶

# SUSSEX

## SUSSEX COUNTY CRICKET CLUB
County Cricket Ground
Eaton Road, Hove, East Sussex, BN3 3AN

☎ (01273) 827100 for general enquiries
(01273) 827145 for prospects of play

**www**.sussexcricket.co.uk
**Email:** info@sussexcricket.co.uk

### Getting there
The County Cricket Ground is half a mile from Hove railway station: if you use services from London and the South-east, you will have to change at Brighton. Buses 6, 6A, 7 and 7A run from Brighton station to Hove station and many other Brighton buses go close to the ground
☎ (01273) 206666 for further information.

There is a buzz around the Hove ground. The club won the double in 2006 (the County Championship and the C&G Trophy) and a major redevelopment of the ground is planned, thanks to a legacy of £11 million left by Spen Cama, a past president. New stands will block the view of residents in the famous tall apartment blocks that overlook the ground. One of the flats once belonged to Ron Greenwood, the former England and West Ham United football manager, though he was never seen in the cricket ground. The redevelopment will include a museum that will be open to all spectators, not just members. At present archivist Rob Boddie keeps a wealth of material in a portakabin near the Arthur Gilligan stand at the Sea End of the ground. It includes a complete set of Wisden (John Wisden played for Sussex) and many other books, along with a 1974 blazer worn by Tony Greig.

Sussex is the oldest English county club, formed in 1839. The club played at the Royal Brunswick Ground – now Fourth Avenue – in Hove. When the club moved to Eaton Road in 1871 the turf was dug up and transported to the new site, where the inaugural first class match was played against Gloucestershire in 1872. The pavilion was built in the 1880s and has been enlarged, improved and developed throughout the twentieth century.

In the members' pavilion, the committee room has paintings and photographs of past players, including George Cox, CB Fry, Arthur Gilligan, Sir Aubrey Smith, Prince Ranjitsinhji and Maurice Tate. It's an eclectic mix: Aubrey Smith was an actor as well as a player, and helped found a cricket club in Hollywood for English actors making films there. Kumar Shri Ranjitsinhji, who became the Maharaja of Nawanagar in 1907, was an explosive cricketer who

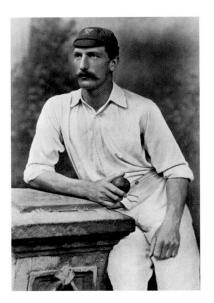

*Right,
Aubrey Smith,
founder of
Hollywood CC.*

*Below left,
Kumar Shri Ranjitsintji
Cambridge University
and Sussex.*

*Below right,
CB Fry.*

developed a new style of batting: in the early twentieth century, most batsmen played off the front foot, but Ranji perfected the back foot style and, with it, the leg glance.

The Jim Parks Bar in the pavilion has a display of blazers, caps and bats owned by the late Reverend David Sheppard, and a tribute to the Parks family: Harry, Jim Senior and Jim Junior all played for the county. Sussex is a family club in every way: another family of players, James, John and Richard Langridge, are also commemorated. A wooden plaque marks the contribution made to the game by William Lillywhite (1792-1854), who was the father of round-arm bowling and is buried in Highgate Cemetery in north London. In Dexter's Restaurant, named after the flamboyant Sussex and England cricketer 'Lord' Ted Dexter, there is an honours board listing all of the club's captains and the Gillette Cup pennants won in 1963 and 1964. Much of all this fascinating material will be moved into the planned museum.

## HYNDMAN: CRICKETING MARXIST

HM (Henry Myers) Hyndman, 1842-1922, was an unlikely player for Sussex during the nineteenth century. Hyndman was a convert to Marxism and, with William Morris and Marx's daughter, Eleanor, created the first Marxist organisation in Britain, the Social Democratic Federation, in 1881. His contribution to Sussex was modest, with a batting average of 16, though he did score 58 in a match against Hampshire at Hove in 1864. No doubt Hyndman would have approved in his time of gentlemen and players leaving the dressing room for the pitch from different gates: no fraternisation between the bourgeoisie and the proletariat.

*Left,
Marxist Sussex crick-
eter, HM Hyndman.*

*Below,
Sussex's Mushtaq
Ahmed lifts the trophy
after his team beat
Lancashire in 2006
in the Cheltenham &
Gloucester Trophy
final at Lord's.*

### GREAT FEATS

✶ Pride of place must go to Mushtaq Ahmed who in 2006 took 100 wickets for the county and was instrumental in helping Sussex to win the County Championship.

✶ The most astonishing batting at Hove came from Notts player Ted Alletson in 1911: he scored 189 in 90 minutes, with the last 142 runs coming in 40 minutes after lunch. Alletson hit the unfortunate Sussex bowler Killick for 34 in one over, a feat not beaten until 1968 when Gary Sobers scored 36 off Malcolm Nash's bowling at Swansea (see Glamorgan section).

✶ The highest innings total for Sussex was 670 for 9 declared against Northants in 1921, while the highest individual innings was a triple Nelson – 333 – by KS Duleepsinghji, also against the unfortunate Northants in 1930.

✶ Best bowling performance for Sussex was by the amazingly initialled JEBBPQC Dwyer, who took 9 for 35 against Derbyshire in 1906. Dwyer had a match total of 16 for 100 in the same game. The batsmen were probably too busy working out what his initials stood for to watch his deliveries with due care and attention.

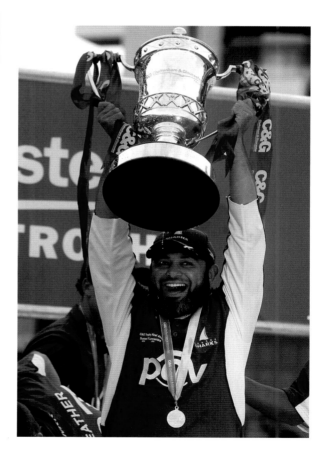

*Left,
Ted Dexter,
captain of Sussex
and England,
in action for his club
in 1963.*

*Below,
Sussex players
celebrate the wicket
of Leicestershire's
George Walker
during the
Frizzell County
Championship
division one match
at the County Ground
in Hove, Sussex.*

## Recommended Pubs HOVE

### SUSSEX CRICKETER
Eaton Road, East Sussex, BN3 3AF

☼ 12-11 (midnight Thu to Sat); 11-11 Sun
☎ (01273) 771645

What a brilliant entrance to a cricket ground, a pub that stands next to the gates, with a garden inside them. The pub was originally a hotel in the 1870s and was used by players, who mixed socially with spectators. Today the Cricketer is a spacious open-plan tavern with many tucked away nooks and crannies, and some modern paintings on the wall. It is part of the Ember Inns chain, which in turn is a specialist group within the giant national pub company Mitchells & Butlers. My local in St Albans, the King William IV, comes from the same chain so the Hove menu was familiar to me: steaks, fish and pasta with several vegetarian options: food is served all day until 9pm. Ember Inns specialises in a rolling programme of beers drawn mainly from regional brewers. On my visit the superb Harveys Sussex Best Bitter from nearby Lewes was available, along with Greene King IPA and Timothy Taylor Landlord.

## BRIGHTON

### WAGGON AND HORSES
109 Church Street, BN1 2PS

✪ 11-11; 12-10.30 Sun
☎ (01273) 602752

A short, pleasant stroll or bus ride along the sea front brings you to the cosmopolitan pleasures of Brighton. Don't be put off by the garish lager umbrellas that cover the outside seating area at the Waggon & Horses. Inside this is a well-scrubbed and unspoilt pub that dates from 1848, though it was originally built as a gymnasium two years earlier. The Waggon has one long bar with bare boards and half-panelled walls decorated with seascapes and an old pub sign for the Volunteers, and there's plenty of seating despite the small size of the room. Food is served at lunchtime and the beers include Adnams Broadside, Fuller's London Pride, Harvey's Sussex Best and the Czech Budweiser Budvar on draught. The pub is handy for the Theatre Royal and in warm weather is a pleasant to sit outside, if you don't mind those umbrellas.

### EVENING STAR
55-56 Surrey Street, BN1 3PB

✪ 12 (11.30 Sat) to 11 (midnight Fri & Sat); 12-11 Sun
☎ (01273) 328931
www. eveningstarbrighton.co.uk

This is a must-visit pub, a beer drinkers' Mecca just 400 yards from Brighton railway station. On a hot summer's afternoon it was my final port of call and at first I thought it must be closed as nobody was sitting outside. I cautiously tried the door: it was open and inside the pub was heaving. It has scrubbed floors, walls settles and bare brick walls, while the small bar in the corner dispenses many delights: this pub is owned by the Dark Star brewery in Ansty, West Sussex, and serves its superb Hophead, Original and seasonal beers: Hophead is well named and its bitter hop character will leaves creases in your tongue. There is a range of guest beers from other craft breweries and draught cider, while a board lists Belgian and German imports. This is such a shrine to quality beer that a man wearing a Beck's T-shirt was asked (jokingly) what he was doing there. Beer festivals are held regularly (consult the website) and there is live music on Sundays.

**Other Cricket Grounds**
*Sussex also plays at Arundel,
Eastbourne, Hastings
and Horsham*

## ARUNDEL

### ARUNDEL CASTLE CRICKET CLUB
Arundel Park,
West Sussex, BN18 9LH

☎ (01903) 882462
(including prospects of play)

**King's Arms**
36 Tarrant Street, BN18 9DN

✪ 11-3, 5.30-11; 11-11 Sat;
12-10.30 Sun
☎ (01903) 882312

**Beers:** Fuller's London Pride,
Hop Back Summer Lightning,
Young's Special and guest beers.

❀ ◖ ⊞ ⅄ ⇌ ♣

## EASTBOURNE

### EASTBOURNE CRICKET CLUB
The Saffrons,
Compton Place Road
Eastbourne, East Sussex,
BN21 1EA

☎ (01323) 724328 (including
prospects of play)

**Buccaneer**
10 Compton Street, BN21 4BW

✪ 11-11, 12-10.30 Sun
☎ (01323) 732829

**Beers:** Draught Bass, Greene King
Abbot, Tetley Bitter and
guest beers.

◖ ◗ ⇌

## HASTINGS

### HASTINGS AND ST LEONARD'S PRIORY CRICKET CLUB
The Pavilion
Bohemia Road, St Leonard's-on-Sea,
Hastings, East Sussex,
TN34 1EX

☎ (01424) 424546
(including prospects of play)

**First In Last Out**
14 High Street, Old Town
Hastings, TN34 3ET

✪ 11-11; 12-10.30 Sun
☎ (01424) 425079
www. thefilo.co.uk

Home of the FILO micro-brewery.

**Beers:** FILO Crofters, Ginger Tom
and Gold (summer).

⚒ Q ❀ ◖ ⅄ ♣

*Arundel Castle Cricket Club provides an
attractive setting for Sussex matches.*

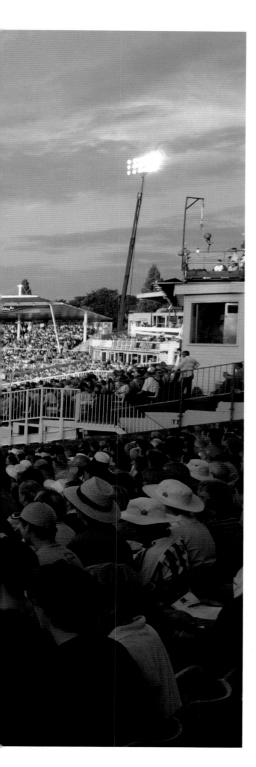

## WARWICKSHIRE

### WARWICKSHIRE COUNTY CRICKET CLUB
The County Ground
Edgbaston, Birmingham, West Midlands, B5 7QU

☎ (0121) 446 4422 (including prospects of play)
www.thebears.co.uk
Email: info@edgbaston.com

### Getting There
Birmingham New Street railway station is approximately two miles away. You can get a taxi to the ground but you will need to extend your overdraft facility as £1.20 is on the clock before you have cleared the station. Buses 45 and 47 link the station, city centre and the ground.

Cricket was first recorded in Birmingham in the mid-eighteenth century when the landlord of the Bell Inn in Smallbrook advertised for teams to play his pub side. Dozens of small clubs sprang up in the city in the following years: a county side was established in 1882 and reorganised two years later. Edgbaston was acquired as the home base in 1886 and was the third ground used by the club. The key person involved in raising the funds to buy the land was William Ansell, who has a stand named in his honour. I had hoped that he was a member of the Ansell brewing family in Aston but William turned out be a schoolmaster. Edgbaston was rough meadowland belonging to Lord Calthorpe, who leased it to the players and a library behind the Ansell Stand bears his name. The club is generous in honouring past players and benefactors and there are stands named after Eric Hollies, RES Wyatt, RV Ryder, Stanley Barnes and Leslie Deakins. The Wicket Gate at the Pavilion End is dedicated to Sydney Barnes and carries an inscription that says the gate marks the spot where he entered the ground in 1894 to play in his first county match. 'Universally acknowledged in later years as "the greatest bowler of them all", it seemed appropriate to the committee of the Warwickshire County Cricket Club to perpetuate his memory at this point where his county career commenced and his ashes now rest.'

Edgbaston always looks rather bleak on television but this is due to the fact that it has a capacity of 21,000, which is only reached when Test Matches or One-Day Internationals are staged there. In real life, the ground is remarkably cosy and friendly, with cheerful and welcoming staff at the entrances. Edgbaston has been overhauled and redeveloped in recent years, starting with the Wyatt Stand in the 1990s and followed by the Cricket Centre that was finished in time for the new century and has excellent facilities for training young players. Two years later the Rea Bank Stand was redeveloped as the Eric Hollies Stand at a cost of £2 million. In 2002 Edgbaston celebrated 100 years as a Test Match venue and it now regularly stages World Cup and One-Day Internationals. A crowd of 15,000 watched the first ever day/night game in 1997 against Somerset.

The museum is in the pavilion complex but is not restricted to members. It is open on match days: contact the club for further information. This is one of the best museums in the country, with a wealth of material. There is the inevitable library of Wisdens and a collection of bats, including the one used by

Brian Lara when he scored 501 not out in 1994. A collection of cartoons by Norman Edwards, who covered the fortunes and misfortunes of the club in several Birmingham newspapers, occupy one corner. George Paine's MCC blazer and cap mark his tour of the West Indies during 1934 and 1935. Paine took 155 wickets in the 1934 season, which is a club record, and a total of 962 wickets during his career at an average of 22.73. There is a bust of Septimus Kinneir who scored 268 against Hampshire at Edgbaston in 1911. Many photographs of touring teams are also displayed but pride of place, in a special cabinet, goes to the England and Australian teams who played in the epic Edgbaston Test in 2005, which England won by two runs. There is a

*Above, Warwickshire's Eric Hollies took 2,323 wickets during his 25-year career.*

*Right, Sydney Barnes, to whom the Wicket Gate is dedicated.*

---

**GREAT FEATS**

✴ Pride of place must go to Brian Lara's monumental 501 not out against Durham in 1994. Not surprisingly, the highest innings total scored by the county was in the same match: 810. Twenty years previously, in 1974, John Jameson and Rohan Kanhai scored 465 against Gloucestershire.

✴ In 1946 Eric Hollies took 10 wickets for 49 against Notts, while TL Pritchard took 14 for 93 against Glamorgan in a match in 1951.

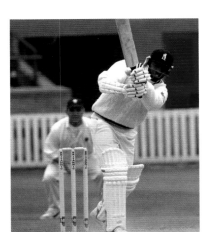

*Left, Brian Lara batting for Warwickshire against Somerset in 1998.*

mounted ball used in the game and two bats signed by both teams.

Eric Hollies features strongly in the museum: there are MCC touring blazers, including the tour of the West Indies in 1934 and 1935, during which he took seven wickets for 50 runs in one Test. There is a statue of Hollies and photographs of his last match at Edgbaston against Surrey in 1957. In a career that ran from 1932 to 1957, he took 2,323 wickets. Team photographs from 1894 to the present day are on display along with individual portraits of Tom Dollery, Norman Gifford, Brian Lara, Alan Smith, MJK Smith, Bob Willis and RES Wyatt.

*Left, A happy crowd at Edgbaston.*

## EDGBASTON: THE GREATEST TEST ?

In August 2005, England beat Australia to level the Ashes series. That is the bald fact, but it disguises a game of drama, nail-biting tension and a final victory that caused Richie Benaud to describe it as one of the most thrilling games he had ever seen. On the final day it seemed that Australia were dead and buried, and an England victory assured. With only two wickets to fall, Australia could have attempted to occupy the crease and block, but Shane Warne and Brett Lee decided to go down fighting. Warne, who had already taken 10 wickets in the match, scored 42 off 59 balls. When he had the misfortune to step on his wicket, it seemed the game must end quickly as the last batsman, Kasprowicz, had the reputation of being a rabbit. But with Lee he put on 59 for the last wicket until he gloved a catch off Harmison to Geraint Jones behind the wicket. Lee was undefeated on 43 and the enduring memory of the game is the image of England captain Andrew Flintoff commiserating with Lee, who had sunk to the ground in complete dejection.

England won by two runs, the narrowest victory in Test history. Flintoff scored 73 in the second England innings and then took three vital Australian wickets: he was named Man of the Match but in truth all 22 players should have been given the accolade. And was Kasprowicz genuinely out caught behind? Don't ask...

## Recommended Pubs
# BIRMINGHAM

### OLD FOX
54 Hurst Street, B5 4TD

☢ 11.20-midnight (2am Thu to Sat); 12-midnight Sun
☎ (0121) 622 5080

This imposing pub, a short walk from New Street, is opposite the Hippodrome Theatre and displays its theatrical connections with old posters in both connecting bars: they range from Shakespeare to opera and ballet. There are many photographs of the stars that have appeared at the theatre, including Charles Chaplin, who is reputed to have drunk in the pub. The front bar is small and bare boarded while the lounge is spacious and carpeted with ample seating, including padded wall seats. Leaded windows have a fox motif while a CAMRA map on one wall helpfully details a pub crawl of Birmingham and West Midlands hostelries. Food is available at lunchtime and in the evening and includes a matinee menu for theatregoers. An excellent range of handpumped beers includes Everard's Tiger, Greene King Old Speckled Hen, Marston Pedigree, St Austell Tribute and Tetley Bitter. There are pavement seats for summer drinking.

❀ ◖ ◗ ♿ ⇌ (New St) ⎚

### OLD JOINT STOCK
4 Temple Row West, B2 5NY

☢ 11-11; closed Sun
☎ (0121) 200 1892

Before we get on to the beer, this is one of the most visually stunning pubs in the country. It stands opposite St Philip's Cathedral and was built in 1864 to a design by the leading Victorian architect Julius Alfred Chatwin. The Grade II listed building was originally the Joint Stock Bank, which was taken over by Lloyds in 1889. It became a Fuller's Ale & Pie House in 1997. The illuminated exterior has pilasters and Roman statuettes while the vast, two-storey interior has colonnades, huge windows with rouched curtains, maroon-painted walls with photographs of old Birmingham, and a vast central bar built with carved wood and topped by a mighty cupola. The former bank manager's office at the rear is now the Club Room while the assistant manager's office is the gent's toilet: here was a man who knew his place. The area at the back has one of the all-time great pub signs: 'To the Ladies and Disabled Lavatories'. I hope they get around to repairing them. Excellent value and good quality food is served from noon until 8pm and follows the Fuller's theme with a range of pies, including the classic steak and ale. The bar serves the full range of Fuller's beers: Chiswick Bitter, Discovery, London Pride, ESB and seasonal ales, and often has beers from the local Beowulf Brewery. It is one of the biggest sellers of London Pride in the Fuller's estate: in fact, it has on occasion been the biggest seller of the beer. This flies in the face of the opinion that when the brewer opened a pub in Birmingham, nobody would drink a beer with London in its name. There are rooms on the first floor that can be used for meetings and social functions, and one room has been developed as an 80-seat theatre. Go and marvel.

## WELLINGTON
37 Bennetts Hill, B2 5SN

☎ (0121) 200 3115
www.thewellingtonrealale.co.uk

The Wellington is owned by Black Country Ales of Dudley and is simply amazing: it is dedicated to cask beer to the exclusion of all else. No food is served, though customers can take their own and the pub even makes cutlery available. There are no fewer than 14 handpumps on the long bar. Rather like a Chinese restaurant, you order beers by numbers: they are displayed on screens on the wall. The choice is mind-boggling: Black Country's Bradley's Finest Golden, Pig on the Wall and Fireside along with Archer's, Brown Cow, Eastwood, E&S, Hydes, Smiles, Springhead, Wold Top, Tom Wood, Tower and Wye Valley. But the range changes all the time. The pub is one long room, narrow by the entrance with a wider, carpeted area at the back. Black Country were told they would never make a success of a pub in this part of Birmingham as there was too much competition from night clubs and youth venues. But it has been packed from day one and sold more than 2,000 different beers in 2005. It's no surprise that it was named CAMRA's local pub of the year in 2006. The Wellington backs on to the Old Joint Stock and you can go from one pub to the other via rear entrances. Both pubs are handy for New Street and Snow Hill stations and both are worth missing a few trains for.

**Q** ♿ ⇌ (New St/ Snow Hill) ⊖ (Snow Hill) 🚌 🍎

*If you can't bear to leave Edgbaston, the Midlands Arts Centre in Cannon Hill Park opposite the cricket ground is a leisure complex with a bar that always serves two cask beers. See the website www.macarts.org.uk.

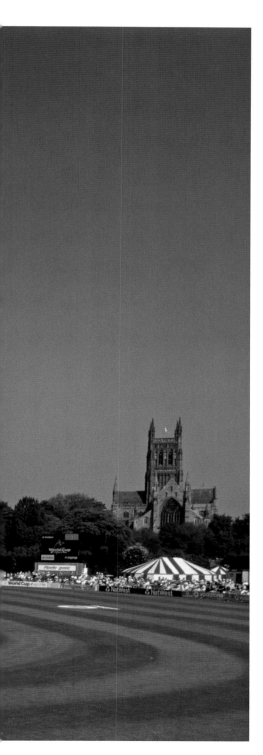

## WORCESTERSHIRE

### WORCESTERSHIRE COUNTY CRICKET CLUB
County Ground, New Road, Worcester, WR2 4QQ

☎ (including prospects of play) (01905) 748474
www.wccc.co.uk
Email: webmaster@wccc.co.uk

### Getting there
Worcester Foregate Station is half a mile from the ground;
Worcester Shrub Hill Station one mile.
Buses 23, 24, 25, 26, 33, 44 and 46 link Angel Place, close to
Foregate Station, with the ground.

New Road is without doubt the most pleasing ground to the eyes of
spectators. The intimate playing area, the stands and pavilion are all
individually and collectively, attractive, but it is the backdrop of the city's four-
teenth-century cathedral that turns a cricket ground into a visual delight. I have
played several times in Verulam Park in St Albans, with the Abbey cathedral
soaring above the pitches, but while the view is spectacular, I have to admit
the quality of cricket could not match that at Worcester.

Cricket teams had been playing in and around Worcester from the
1840s, but a formal club in the city was not launched until 1865 at a
meeting in the Star Hotel. The local nobility and gentry were there in force
and their style can be measured by the notes of a meeting in 1866 that
recorded expenditure of sixteen shillings for 'hire of horse and man, two
days rolling'. The horse came first. The players soon came to realise they
needed to broaden the base of the club. The City of Worcester club
merged with another local team in the 1850s and set about attracting factory workers to augment their number. Social distinctions prevailed, however. The minutes of the merged club noted that 'five shilling members' could
play with bats and balls two nights a week and could play with the 'half
guinea' members one night of the week.

The county club played first at Broughton Park, where Paul Foley, an
ironmaster from Stourbridge, became the driving force. He organised the
first Minor Counties Championship, which Worcestershire duly won in
1895, 1896, 1897 and 1898. Fired with success, the club applied for
First Class status and moved in 1899 to New Road, on land rented by
Foley from the Dean and Chapter of the cathedral. A pavilion was built
that year and the inaugural First Class county game was staged in May
against Yorkshire. Dressed in formal clothes, Foley helped finish painting
the sightscreens on the morning of the game.

*Right, Worcestershire team group in 1964: (back row, l-r) Alan Ormrod, Norman Gifford, Basil D'Oliveira, Len Coldwell, Ron Headley, Doug Slade; (front row, l-r) Tom Graveney, Jack Flavell, Don Kenyon, Martin Horton, Dick Richardson, Roy Booth.*

The Foster Room in the pavilion commemorates the remarkable contribution made to the club in its early years by the Foster family, seven of whose sons played at New Road. Their father, the Reverend Harry Foster, taught at Malvern College. A copper beech tree at the cathedral end of the ground was planted to mark Don Kenyon's long career with the club, including playing in the first County Championship team in 1964, an achievement repeated the following year. The Basil D'Oliveira stand is a tribute to the player who courageously helped end the cruel divisions in South Africa during the apartheid era.

As well as its attractiveness, New Road also has the reputation of being the wettest ground in the country. The rivers Teme and Severn flood it regularly and as a result boating, fishing, swimming and even ice-skating have taken place there. Fortunately floods usually only occur during the winter and early spring.

A brass plate in the pavilion measures the highest water level of flooding in 1947, several feet above the playing area.

The ground, which has a capacity of 8,500, has been improved in recent years, with a new roof for the New Road Stand, executive boxes, and a modern shop and reception area. World Cup matches were staged there in 1999 and the installation of floodlighting has enabled day/night and Twenty20 games to take place.

The old Ladies' Pavilion is open to the public on match days and has a collection of cricket books, photos of games in progress and of players from the nineteenth century to the present day. The photos include Graeme Hick, one of the most prolific scorers in the history of the game, making his Test debut for England in 1993. The pavilion, which is for members only, has further old team photos, trophies, ancient bats and old wicketkeepers' gloves.

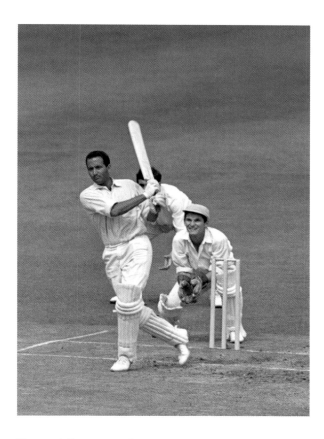

*Above,*
*The South African*
*Basil D'Oliveira*
*joined Worcestershire*
*in 1964.*
*Left, Basil D'Oliveira*
*in batting action for*
*the MCC.*

*Below, Worcestershire*
*Royals' Graeme Hick*
*in action against*
*Somerset Sabres*
*during a 2006*
*Twenty20 Cup match*
*at the County Cricket*
*Ground, Worcester.*

*Above,*
*Don Kenyon –*
*a copper beech tree*
*was planted*
*at the ground to*
*mark his long*
*career with*
*the county.*

### Beer at the ground

Handpumped beer is available in the members' dining room and includes Bumpy's Brew, a house name for Jenning's Cumberland Ale, and Marston's Pedigree.

---

### GREAT FEATS

✳Pride of place goes to Graeme Hick, who scored 315 not out against Durham in 2002. Hick has also taken part in two outstanding partnerships: 300 with WPC Weston against the Indian touring side in 1996, and 205 with PJ Newport against Yorkshire in 1988.

✳Tom Graveney, partnered by MJ Horton, put together a stand of 314 against Somerset in 1962.

✳In 1931, CF Root took nine wickets for just 23 against Lancashire.

✳RTD Perks took 15 wickets for 106 against Essex in 1937.

*Worcester Cathedral looms over the County Ground.*

**Recommended Pubs**
## WORCESTER

**BELL**
35 St John's, WR2 5AG

✪ 10.30-2; 5-11 (11.30 Fri); 10.30-4, 7-11 Sat;
12-3, 7-11 Sun
☎ (01905) 424570

This delightful local opposite St John's Church is a short
walk from the cricket ground. It has wattle and daub walls
in the main bar that are decorated with old theatre bills
marking visits to the city by the Beatles, Roy Orbison and
Maurice Chevalier. There is a fascinating giant jigsaw
made from the front page of The People newspaper in
1966, showing Bobby Moore (yet again) holding up the
World Cup as he is carried by his team-mates. It's a good
job England won the Ashes in 2005, as English football
hasn't had much to celebrate for 40 years. The pub is
popular with the St John's cycling club, one of two smaller
rooms off the main bar can be used by families and there
is also a skittles alley. The range of beers is excellent: that
old Brummie stalwart M&B Brew XI is accompanied by
guest beers that may include Cannon Royal Muzzle
Loader, St George's Paragon Steam from a Worcester
brewery and Fuller's London Pride.

 ♣

## BUSH
4 Bull Ring, St Johns, WR2 5AD

☼ 10.30-3; 5.30-11; 10.30-11 Sat;
   7-10.30 Sun
☎ (01905) 421086

The key feature of this imposing Victorian pub, closer to the ground than the Bell, is the ornate, carved and curved bar in the main room, which also has etched and stained glass windows. There is a fine gantry behind the bar with a wind-up clock and service to the lounge at the rear through a hatch. The back room, called Mulbury's Restaurant, serves steaks, chicken dishes, fish and chips and vegetarian options and opens in the evenings from 5.30 – 9.30. The main pub has bar lunches and all-day breakfasts. The main beer is Banks's Bitter from Wolverhampton, with a good range of guest beers such as Greene King's Ruddles County, Old Speckled Hen and Abbot Ale, plus Wells' Bombardier. I pointed out to the landlord that one of his smaller bars carries the inscription 'Smoke Room'. 'We're working on that,' he said. As a full ban on smoking comes into operation in 2007, this bar will become a memorial to nicotine's past.

▶ ◖ ⊞

## CRICKETERS
Angel Street, WR1 3QT

☼ 11-11 (midnight Fri & Sat); 12-10.30 Sun
☎ Unlisted

This city-centre pub is a shrine to the game, with signed bats, portraits of the local ground, and cartoons of Worcestershire heroes, including Tom Graveney, Graeme Hick and Basil D'Oliveira. The large single room has been knocked through from several smaller ones and has a commanding horseshoe bar, beamed ceiling and carpeted floor. A substantial menu is available lunchtime and evening, and there is a good range of beers: Black Sheep Best Bitter, Deuchar's IPA, Greene King Ruddles County and Shepherd Neame Spitfire. It's a cosy and welcoming pub and a good place to spend an hour if the heavens open and rain stops play.

◖ ▶

# YORKSHIRE

## YORKSHIRE COUNTY CRICKET CLUB

Headingley, Leeds, West Yorkshire, LS6 3BU

☎ (0113) 278 7394 (including prospects of play)
www.yorkshireccc.org.uk
Email: cricket@yorkshireccc.org.uk

### Getting There

**Trains** are every 30 minutes from Central station to Headingley on the Harrogate line, followed by five minutes' walk to the ground.
**Buses** 38, 56, 18, 18a, 91 and 91a run from Leeds city centre, and buses 74, 75, 76 and 77 run from Central railway station to the ground.

The Headingley ground has changed out of all recognition in recent years. The raucous amphitheatre was famous for its rudimentary concrete benches, but more comfortable and colourful seats have replaced them, while an attractive reception area in the East Stand greets visitors at the Rugby Ground end (the cricket club shares the ground with the Rugby League club). But more changes are in the offing. A few years ago there was talk of Yorkshire leaving Headingley for a new ground in Wakefield, but that has been abandoned. Paul Caddick, the new chairman of the cricket, football and athletic company that owns the land, has invested considerable sums in redeveloping the ground. The West Stand and terracing have been rebuilt at a cost of £32 million. The new East Stands followed and include a hotel, the Headingley Lodge, crickets nets, meeting rooms, reception areas and a large members' bar. There is more work to come too: in the next few years, the old North Stand, which is double sided, one side for viewing cricket, the other for rugby, will be redeveloped and a new pavilion will be built at the Kirkstall Lane End.

At present, the memorabilia at the ground is on view to members only, but further development will include a museum within the next two years, which will enable other material currently held in store to be placed on show for the general public. At present, the staircase of the East Stand has fine portraits of Lord Hawke, Fred Trueman, Wilfred Rhodes, Sir Len Hutton, a painting of a match at Scarborough between Yorkshire and Glamorgan, and a modern portrait of Geoff Boycott by Ken Taylor: when Taylor retired from cricket he took up portrait painting. In 2007, the bat used by Boycott when he scored his 100th century during a Test at Headingley will be taken from Lord's and put on display at his home ground. There will also be a special commemoration to

*Right,
Hedley Verity
Yorkshire and
England.*

*Below,
A young
Geoff Boycott walks
out at Lord's to
open the batting.*

*Opposite page,
Botham leaves the
pitch at Headingley
in 1981 at the end
of the innings.*

mark the 75th anniversary of Holmes and Sutcliffe scoring an astonishing 555 between them against Essex at Leyton in 1932.

The new Long Room has five Test Honours Boards: a player who performs well in a Test at the ground will have his name and performance inscribed on the board overnight. There are cabinets devoted to the achievements of George Hirst and Fred Trueman: they include the stump that marks Trueman's 300th Test wicket. An entire wall is devoted to Hedley Verity who took 14 wickets in a day in 1934 against the Australians at Lords. Verity died on active service with the Green Howards in Italy in 1943 and his death certificate, in Italian, is included in the display. Verity served in the same regiment as another famous Yorkshire player and long-time captain, Norman Yardley.

The Hirst and Rhodes Suite in the Old Pavilion can be used for meetings and entertainment, while members of the England and Wales Cricket Board use the Executive Suite. Across the road, the new Cricket Centre has extensive indoor nets used by both Yorkshire and local clubs. The centre contains a conference room and a cafeteria.

Headlingley is so deeply enshrined in cricket folklore that few people today are aware that the cricket club was founded not in Leeds but in Sheffield in 1863, where it shared the facilities with Sheffield United football club at Bramall Lane. In 1888, wealthy supporters banded together to buy a plot of land in Leeds and formed the Leeds Cricket, Football and Athletic Company. The chairman was Lord Hawke, a formidable figure in Yorkshire and England cricket and who captained the county side from 1883 to 1910. The first major game was played at Headingley in 1890 between the North of England and the touring Australians. A year later Yorkshire CCC staged its first county match with Derby followed by a First-Class match against Kent. Nevertheless, Yorkshire continued to play some matches at Bramall Lane until after World War Two, when the football club needed to redevelop the site.

# HEADINGLEY: BOTHAM'S TEST

My memory of the Monday of the Headingley Test in 1981 is deeply engrained. I happened to be at the head office of CAMRA in St Albans where my old friend and fellow beer writer Barrie Pepper tracked me down. Barrie was watching the match at the ground and his instructions to me were succinct: 'Stop whatever you're doing, go home and watch the cricket on TV.' I did so and saw the amazing drama unfold while, as the news went round Leeds, people started to pour into the ground.

The series against Australia was not going well for England. They were two down when they arrived for the Headingley Test. Botham, after a torrid time in the Lord's Test, had resigned the captaincy, leading to the recall of Mike Brearley. Australia scored more than 400 in their first innings at Headingley and then dismissed England for a paltry 174. England followed on, so by Monday

morning most of the journalists covering the game had booked out of their hotels, thinking that it would all be over within a few hours. This seemed to be a sensible decision as, by late afternoon, England had been reduced to 135 for 7, 92 runs behind. Once wicket keeper Bob Taylor was out, Botham was joined by Graham Dilley, a fast bowler who could bat a bit, but who was not expected to hang around for long. To everyone's surprise, he square cut Terry Alderman for two successive fours. Encouraged by this braggadocio, Botham muttered the immortal words, 'Right, let's give it some humpty' and put Australia to the sword. In the following 80 minutes, Botham and Dilley put on 117 runs. Botham's hitting was pure, not slogging, but so hard that some thought the ball would disintegrate. One hit for six went through a hole in the football stand: it wasn't mended for years. When Dilley was finally out, Botham was joined by Chris Old, who had often dis-

appointed with the bat in Test matches but found sufficient form to put on a further 67. At the close of play, Botham was left with last man Bob Willis.

A day was left and England were 124 ahead. Only five more runs were added and the small crowd expected Australia to knock off 130 runs without difficulty. At 56 for 1, victory seemed certain. Then Bob Willis, bowling from the football stand end, asked to switch ends. He looked like a man in a trance and, bowling with great fire and accuracy, swept the early Aussie batting away. By lunch, Australia were 58 for 4. When the game restarted, Chris Old bowled Allan Border for a duck, and then Willis took two more wickets. Dennis Lillee and Ray Bright staged a fight back, putting on 35 in four overs but finally Australia were dismissed, 20 runs short of victory. It was only the second time in Test history and the first time in the twentieth century that a team had won a Test following on.

*Left, The Len Hutton Gates, cause of some controversy.*

*Opposite top left, The Dickie Bird clock – tribute to a famous umpire.*

*Opposite top right, The Western Terrace at Headingley cost £32 million to construct.*

*Opposite bottom, The new East Stand at Headingley contains a hotel, cricket nets, meeting rooms and a members' bar.*

## GREAT FEATS

★Pride of place here must go to Don Bradman, who was awarded Honorary Life Membership of Yorkshire for his appearances in Tests at Headingley in 1930, 1934, 1938 and 1948. In 1930 he scored 334, made up on the first day of 105 before lunch, 115 between lunch and tea, and 89 in the final session. In 1934, he scored 304.

★The highest innings total for Yorkshire is 560 for 6 declared against Leicestershire in 1921, while the highest individual innings is 270 by Herbert Sutcliffe against Sussex in 1932. In 1928 Holmes and Sutcliffe scored 290 against Middlesex.

★Yorkshire's best bowling performance in an innings is 10 for 10 by Hedley Verity against Notts in 1932, while the best bowling in a match is 15 for 50 by R Peel against Somerset in 1895.

★The largest crowd is 44,507 against Lancashire in 1948: ground capacity today is 20,000 but this will increase with redevelopment.

Headingley has seen some remarkable cricket, such as Bradman's and Botham's feats (see page 141) but the ground is no stranger to controversy. In 1975, when George Davis from the East End of London was convicted of armed robbery, his supporters, who believed he had been framed, staged a series of protests that included digging up the Test wicket at the ground. In 2001 the new Sir Leonard Hutton Gates at the Kirkstall Lane End were greeted with criticism in some newspapers as they showed, among others, women dressed in formal Muslim clothes. The club, anxious to reach out to all members of the local community, has stood firm against such crude attacks. Fortunately, a clock erected in honour of Dickie Bird has not met with any disapproval.

### Beer at the Ground

Draught Caledonian Deuchar's IPA is available in the cafeteria at the new Cricket Centre.

## ARCADIA ALE & WINE BAR

Arndale Centre, Otley Road, Headingley, LS6 2UE

☼ 11-11; 12-10.30 Sun
☎ (0113) 274 5599

This gem is five minutes from the cricket ground and part of a row of retail outlets. The choice of beer, both British and from overseas, is remarkable. The bar, based in a former bank, is part of the Market Town Taverns group run by CAMRA stalwart Ian Fozard. The Arcadia, with its wooden floors, is small yet spacious and has ample seating on two floors. The walls – including the corridors to the toilets – are decorated with a plethora of brewery and beer posters from home and abroad. Behind the small serving area, one wall is covered in pump clips representing many of the beers that have been sold here over the years. On my visit Acorn Barnsley Bitter and Green Bullet, Black Sheep Best Bitter, Caledonian Deuchar's IPA, Goose Eye Waddler and Timothy Taylor's Landord were on handpump, while pressurised draught beers from abroad included Liefmans Kriek and Frambozen, Warsteiner and Kaltenberg Pilsners from Germany, and Erdinger wheat beer. There is a fine range of imported bottled beers, too, including Belgian Trappist brews. There is no music or fruit machines and imaginative food is served at lunchtime and during the evening. A bus stop a few yards away will take you back into the city centre.

Q ◖ ▶ 🚌

## DR OKELLS

159 Headrow, LS1 5RG

☼ 11-11.30 (12.30am Sat); closed Sun
☎ (0113) 242 9674

Dr Okells is one of a small chain of pubs owned and run by the Isle of Man brewery, Okells. This outlet, opposite the imposing bulk of Leeds Town Hall, is based in the spacious offices of a former assurance company. It is large and ornate, with a downstairs bar area and two mezzanine floors, reached by wooden staircases, which offer comfortable seating in deep leather armchairs. The ground floor bar has tiled floors, ochre painted walls and large windows. Music is of the piped variety but includes Miles Davis, John Coltrane and the young Sinatra. Food includes Greek salad, chilli, steak and onion sandwich, Yorkshire pudding filled with beef and mash, and scampi. I enjoyed a beautifully hoppy Okells Bitter: other beers on offer included Copper Dragon Golden Pippin and Northern Brewing Liberty Bell. The Taps served Anchor Steam Liberty from San Francisco, Liefmans Frambozen raspberry beer from Belgium and Brinkhoff Pilsener from Dortmund. The pub is listed as 'Baroque' in the 2007 Good Beer Guide but the name has since been changed to Dr Okells. Regular beer festivals are staged here.

◖ ⇌ 🚌

## SCARBROUGH HOTEL
Bishopgate Street, LS1 5DY

☻ 11-midnight; 12-10 Sun
☎ (0113) 243 4590

The hotel, which no longer does accommodation, is only one minute away from Central railway station and is the ideal place for a beer on the way to or the return from Headingley. It is a Leeds institution and was the local branch of CAMRA's joint Pub of the Year in 2004 and 2005. The spelling of the name is correct: it is named after Henry Scarbrough, its owner in the nineteenth century. The Scarbrough started life as a medieval manor house and was owned by the Bishop of Bristol in the eighteenth century before becoming a hotel in the nineteenth. When the Queens Hotel opened across the road, the building became a pub and music hall, with the best acts going on to the famous Leeds City Varieties. Today, the sumptuous L-shaped bar has big mirrors, fireplaces, wooden floors, wall settles, leather chairs and both Art Nouveau and Art Deco flourishes in the ceiling lights and leaded windows. There is an extensive menu available all day and there are usually five cask beers on offer. Tetley Bitter is a regular and guest beers include Rooster's Hooligan and Young's Special. There is an annual beer festival held in January and the Yorkshire Ale and Produce Festival in the first week of August.

❀ ◖◗ ♿ ⇌ 🍎

*16 Leeds pubs are listed in the 2007 Good Beer Guide.*

## Other Cricket Grounds
*Yorkshire also plays in Scarborough.*

## SCARBOROUGH CRICKET CLUB
The Pavilion, North Marine Road,
Scarborough, North Yorkshire, YO12 7TJ

☎ (01723) 365625 (including prospects of play)

### New Tavern
131 Falsgrave Road. YO12 5EY

☻ 12-3, 5.30-11.30; 12-midnight Fri & Sat; 12-11.30 Sun
☎ (01723) 366965

**Beer:** Camerons Bitter and guest beers.

⊞ ♿ ⚑ ⇌ ♣ P

### North Riding Hotel
161-163 North Marine Road, YO12 7HY

☻ 12-midnight (1am Fri & Sat); 12-midnight Sun
☎ (01723) 370004

**Beer:** Caledonian Deuchar's IPA, Taylor Landlord and Tetley Bitter.

Q ⛭ ◖◗ ⊞ ⚑ ♣

*Nine Scarborough pubs are listed in CAMRA's Good Beer Guide.*

## SCOTLAND

### GRANGE CRICKET CLUB
Portgower Place, off Raeburn Place, Edinburgh, EH4 1HQ

☎ (0131) 332 2148 (including prospects of play)
(0131) 313 7420 for the Scottish Cricket Union
www.cricketscotland.com
Email admin.scu@btinternet.com

### Getting There
Raeburn Place is approximately 15 minutes' walk from
Waverley railway station and Princes Street.

I have been to the attractive town of Dollar near Stirling several times
(until it moved, the Harviestoun Brewery was based there) and noted
with interest on the outskirts of the town a large ground belonging to
Clackmannanshire County Cricket Club. Further investigation showed
that the first recorded game of cricket in Scotland was 220 years ago in
Schaw Park in Alloa, not a million miles from Dollar. The sport was introduced to Scotland by English troops garrisoned there following the
Jacobite rebellion. Similarly, the oldest recorded cricket club is in Kelso
in the Borders, another garrison town. By 1865, the game had made
sufficient progress for Scotland to beat Surrey at the Oval by 172 runs.
Today there are 200 clubs in Scotland and the game is witnessing
something of a revival in a country where football and rugby dominate
the sporting scene. In 2006, SportScotland invested £317,000 to
improve coaching and develop new talent. The national team is doing
well: in 2004 Scotland won the International Cup in Dubai and the following year won the ICC Trophy, defeating Ireland by 47 runs in
Dublin. Scotland is now 12th in the world One-Day rankings – not far
behind England – and was due to play in the 2007 World Cup in
the West Indies.

Support for the game has always been stronger than media cover-
age would suggest. Friends have told me that when Ian Botham was putting Australia to the sword at Headingley in 1981, bars in working-class
districts of Glasgow, where the fortunes of Celtic and Rangers are usually
the main topic of conversation, were packed with drinkers watching
Botham's derring-do on television. In the Long Room of the pavilion at
Raeburn Place, a photograph shows a crowd of around 9,000 watching
Don Bradman's Australians in 1948. The ground can still attract crowds of
a similar size when touring sides or One-Day Internationals are played
there and mobile seating is brought in.

*Left, Douglas Jardine, one of only two Scotsmen to have captained an England cricket team, shown here with Australia's captain Bill Woodfull at the coin toss on the first day of the 1932-1933 Ashes tour.*

*Below, Scotland's John Blain (left) celebrates with team-mates after securing the wicket of New Zealand's Nathan Astle during their World Cup match at the Grange in Edinburgh. New Zealand won the match by six wickets.*

Highland Brigade, a 1948 match against the Yorkshire Gentlemen, and the 1961 Australian touring team. In the Long Room, as well as the picture of Bradman, there's a signed photograph of the 1961 Australian tourists: spot Richie Benaud with dark hair. The pavilion, Long Room and bar are open to members of the Scottish Cricket Union and members of visiting clubs.

### Beer at the ground

Deuchar's IPA is available in the bar.

---

### GREAT FEATS

✰ The highest innings total scored by Scotland is 411 for 6 declared against Ireland in 1956. The highest individual innings for Scotland is 143 not out by BR Todd against Ireland in 1936.

✰ In 1912, RW Sievwright took 7 wickets for 71 against the Australians.

✰ In limited overs matches, Scotland scored 147 against Surrey in 1999 in the NatWest Trophy and 163 against Bangladesh in the 1999 World Cup.

✰ 5,217 watched Scotland play New Zealand at the Grange in the 1999 World Cup.

---

The game is administered by the Scottish Cricket Union at Ravelston in Edinburgh, but Raeburn Place is the main ground for major games. The tree-lined arena is in an especially attractive area of Edinburgh, close to the Arboretum and Botanical Gardens, and boasts one of the finest, if smallest, pavilions in Britain. It is the home of Grange Cricket Club, founded in 1895: the pavilion was opened that year when Scotland played Gloucestershire. WG Grace turned out for the occasion. The Grange Club now includes hockey, tennis and lacrosse teams, and the main room is mainly devoted to tennis photographs. The stairs at the rear that lead to both the ground floor dressing rooms and the first floor committee room and pavilion balcony, which has superb views of Edinburgh, have cricket team photographs, trophies and other pictures showing Prince Ranjitsinhji, a game between the Grange and Oxford University in 1895, Grange versus the

# BODYLINE: THE SCOTTISH CONNECTION

It's a popular pub quiz question: name the two Scotsmen that have captained England at cricket. Answer: Douglas Jardine and Mike Denness. As the infamous 'Bodyline Tour' to Australia has been mentioned several times in the book, a brief outline here may be of interest.

Don Bradman was seen at the main obstacle to England winning the Ashes during the tour of 1932-33. His brilliant batting on a tour of England in 1930, including 334 in the Leeds Test, had been a sensation and Douglas Jardine, appointed captain for the subsequent tour of Australia, knew Bradman's genius had to be curtailed. Jardine had noted that in the Oval Test Bradman was not comfortable against the fast, short-pitched bowling of Harold Larwood on a damp pitch. Bradman had been hit on the chest by one rising ball.

From this example, Jardine developed his 'leg theory' method of playing, which he proposed on the boat to Australia in prolonged conversations with Larwood and his fellow opening bowler Bill Voce, both from Nottinghamshire. Jardine played county cricket for Surrey and ostentatiously wore a Harlequins cap. He was from a patrician, public school background, has been described as aloof, overbearing and with a well-nurtured dislike of Australians. The dislike was reciprocated. During one Test on the 1932-33 tour, Jardine irritably swatted away some flies from his sweating face and a voice in the crowd yelled: 'Hey, Jardine, leave our flies alone – they're the only Australians that like you.'

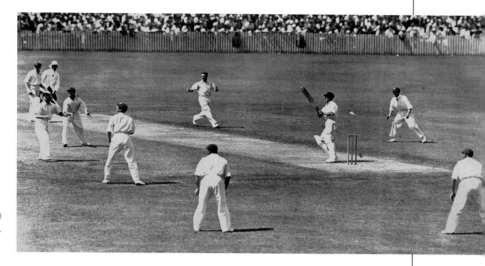

Leg theory or, as Australians called it, Bodyline, entailed Larwood and Voce bowling extremely fast to a packed leg side field. With the ball rearing up at the batsman's body, he would either duck, attempt to hook and give a catch…or get hit. Other members of the touring party, notably Gubby Allen, refused to bowl Bodyline.

Black and white films from the time show astonishing images of Larwood and Voce bowling orthodox balls to a conventional off-side field of slips and gullies. Then, at a signal from Jardine, the close fielders moved from the off to the leg and the bowlers then fired the ball fast and short at the batsmen's leg stump. Although many Australians were hit, only one, Bertie Oldfield, was seriously injured when he was cracked on the head during the Adelaide Test.

Such was the rage at Jardine's tactics that the Australian Board of Control sent a

*England win the Fourth Test Match and regain the Ashes. Left-Right: Verity, Mitchell, Richardson, Wyatt, Larwood, Jardine, Leyland, Sutcliffe and Woodfull.*

cable to MCC at Lord's accusing England of unsporting behaviour. MCC responded by threatening to call off the tour. Like the ball tampering episode at the Oval in 2006, Bodyline had elevated a cricket spat into an international row with political implications. The problem was reputedly discussed at cabinet level by the British government. The tour continued, England won the series 4-1, but Larwood never played for England again and eventually settled, ironically, in Australia. Jardine didn't play for England against Australia again while 'leg theory' was outlawed. Today batsmen wear helmets, chest guards, thigh pads and heavily padded gloves, while close fielders also use helmets and shin guards. Plus ça change…

*Left,*
*Nasser Hassain*
*hits the ball for Essex*
*past Scotland's*
*Douglas Lockhart*
*during the*
*Cheltenham &*
*Gloucester trophy*
*match against at the*
*Grange Cricket.*

## BLUE BLAZER
2 Spittal Street, EH3 9DX

✪ 11 (12.30 Sun) -1am
☎ (0131) 229 5030

*Left,*
*Scotland Fans enjoy*
*the game despite*
*Scotland's defeat.*

The Blue Blazer stands on a busy street corner almost at the foot of the mighty castle that bestrides the area. The eight-teenth-century pub has its history enshrined above the door of the main bar. It was renamed Blue Blazer when it was acquired by Scottish & Newcastle Breweries and pays homage to Heriot School and its dress code: there is a tiled blue blazer built into the wooden floor. The bar is decorated with old whisky prints while a whisky cask stands in the centre and is used as a table. An open fireplace is topped by a wood-framed mirror and a clock from the long-defunct T&J Bernard Brewery, which once owned the bar. The gantry behind the bar is topped by three beer casks with labels announcing the ales available, while a whisky menu indicates the malts and blends on sale. Beyond the main room is a second smaller one with more seating and a collection of malt whisky boxes. Beers include Caledonian Deuchar's IPA and 80 Shilling and such guests as Cairngorm Trade Winds and William Bros Gold.

## CLARK'S BAR
142 Dundas Street, EH3 5DQ

☼ 11-11 (11.30 Thu to Sat); 12.30-11 Sun
☎ (0131) 556 1067

Clark's is a splendid tenement bar handy for Raeburn Place: Dundas Street is the continuation of Hanover Street, a main road of Princes Street, and the best walking route to the cricket ground. The main bar is wood-panelled with button leather wall seats and small glass-topped tables. The walls are decorated with old brewery and whisky mirrors. Two smaller rooms at the rear have many fascinating photographs of old Edinburgh. Behind the long wood bar there is an impressive gantry bursting with a vast range of whiskies. On the bar, Tennent's lager wins the prize for the most garish fount in the known universe. Of greater interest, Caledonian 80 Shilling and McEwan 80 Shilling are served by air pressure founts, a Scottish system now in sad decline as a result of the widespread adoption of the Sassenach handpump, used here to serve Deuchar's IPA. The term shilling is a Victorian system used in Scotland for invoicing beer: the stronger the beer – ranging from 60 Shilling to 80 Shilling – the higher the price.

## OXFORD BAR
8 Young Street, EH2 4JB

☼ 11-1am; 12.30-midnight Sun
☎ (0131) 539 7119
**www**.oxfordbar.com

The Oxford is a New Town institution, just a short walk from Princes Street. A haunt of Edinburgh literati since the nineteenth century, it has achieved more recent fame as a result of appearing in Ian Rankin's gritty Inspector Rebus novels. The pub is also popular with Rugby spectators and can be crowded when important games are played at Murrayfield. Described in the dry local humour as 'a scout hut for the over 30s', the Oxford has a plain exterior leading into a small front room with a long bar and space for no more than a few regulars. The bar's gantry is packed with whisky bottles interspersed with memorabilia of Robert Burns. To the right, a bigger room, where walls are crowded with an eclectic mix of photographs, has space for those seeking basic creature comforts. Caledonian Deuchar's IPA is the house beer and you may find Belhaven 80 Shilling, Edinburgh EPA or other guest ales. Snacks include Falkirk Pies and bridies, a Scottish version of the Cornish pastie. The Oxford is on CAMRA's National Inventory of pubs with historic interiors. It's a gem.

*There are 20 Edinburgh pubs listed in the Good Beer Guide.*

## CRICKET LOVERS' GUIDE TO BEER

There's beer...and then there's real ale. This book is dedicated to a style of beer that has been saved from extinction by CAMRA, the Campaign for Real Ale. It's a style that's also known as cask-conditioned beer or cask beer for short. Whatever it's called, it's natural beer, living beer. The beers and lagers produced by giant national and global companies are filtered and pasteurised before they leave their breweries and are then served by applied gas pressure. They are often made with cheap grains such as rice and corn, with inferior hops.

Real ale, on the other hand, is a living product that leaves the brewery in an unfinished state and reaches maturity in casks in pub cellars. It's brewed from the finest barley malts, hops, yeast and water and is kept in good condition in the cask by carbon dioxide created by fermentation, not gas from a cylinder. The natural gas gives the beer its sparkle in the glass and helps create a lively head of foam.

The brewing process is time-honoured: barley malt, often a blend of pale malt and darker varieties for colour and flavour, is mixed in a large vessel called a mash tun with pure hot water. The porridge-like mixture, known as the mash, is left to stand for an hour or two and during that time enzymes in the malt convert barley starch into fermentable sugar. The sugary extract, called wort, is run off from the base of the tun and pumped to another vessel called the copper. Here it is boiled vigorously for an hour or more with hops, which add bitterness. There are many varieties of hops: some are used for their bitterness, others for their delightful piny, resiny, grassy, spicy, peppery and citrus fruit characteristics. Hops also contain acids and tannins that help keep beer free from infection.

When the copper boil is finished, the liquid – hopped wort – is cooled and then pumped to fermenting vessels, where it is thoroughly mixed with yeast. Every brewery has its own 'house yeast' that adds its own distinctive character to the beer. In the fermenter, the yeast vigorously turns malt sugars into alcohol and carbon dioxide, creating at the same time rich biscuity and fruity flavours. After about seven days, fermentation is complete. The beer is kept in conditioning tanks for a day or two to purge itself of rough alcohols and is then run or 'racked' into casks, often with the addition of a handful of fresh hops for aroma and some brewing sugar to encourage a powerful second fermentation in cask.

Casks are set up in pub cellars and 'tapped', which means porous pegs of wood are knocked through venting holes in the tops of the casks to allow the beer to breathe and vent off some of the gas produced by the secondary fermentation. Lines or plastic tubes are attached to bung holes at the front of the casks and linked to beer engines and handpumps on the pub bar. Finings, a clearing agent, have been added to the casks in the brewery: they attract yeast and proteins in the beer, dragging them to the foot of each cask. When the beer is judged to have 'dropped bright' it is served by operating the handpump on the bar, which opens a beer engine or suction pump beneath the bar and draws the beer from the cask to the glass. The recommended serving temperature is 11 to 12 degrees Celsius.

Real ale comes in a variety of styles – mild, bitter, best bitter, extra special bitter, old ale, barley wine, golden ale, harvest ale, porter and stout. All are linked to a method of brewing as traditional and noble as the game of cricket. Cask beer is brewed by regional and family-owned breweries and by a growing army of smaller 'micro breweries' now numbering more than 500. They are all listed in the annual CAMRA Good Beer Guide.

You can support CAMRA's work to protect real ale and encourage more breweries to make it by joining its ranks of 85,000 members: see the membership form in the back of this book. Membership will also enable you to enter the private members' clubs mentioned in the book that will admit you if you show a CAMRA membership card or a copy of the Good Beer Guide.

*Opposite page: Caledonian Brewery's cricket team, seen at Lord's, plays a competitive series called The Mashes with other brewery teams.*

*Barley Wine*

*IPA*

*Extra Special Bitter*

*Mild*

*Stout*

*Bitter*

# Postscript: WHAT HAPPENED AT HAMBLEDON?

Cricket returned to Hambledon in the twentieth century. As a result of the demise of the Hambledon club at the end of the eighteenth century, Broadhalfpenny Down reverted to agricultural use, but in 1908 interest in the famous old ground revived when a stone was erected to mark its enormous contribution to the game. The stone was unveiled during a match between an England XII, captained by Gilbert Jessop, and a Hambledon team that included the legendary all-rounder CB Fry.

Occasional games were played at the ground until Winchester College bought it in 1925 to preserve its cricketing heritage and to encourage regular games to be played there. During the 1930s, the ground was leased to Wadham Brothers, a local engineering firm, for use as their sports ground. The managing director, William Wadham, was a keen sportsmen and he helped organise a number of matches at Broadhalfpenny, some attended by prominent sportsmen. Following World War Two and a period of economic austerity, Wadhams were no longer able to justify the expenditure the ground demanded and they relinquished the lease.

Fortunately, the Royal Navy stepped into the breach. HMS Mercury, the Navy's Signal School, had moved to Leydene House, a mile from Broadhalfpenny, during the war, and sailors and civilians stationed there played occasional matches on the down. As a result, HMS Mercury took on the lease in 1952. In 1959, a group of Mercury's officers formed the Broadhalfpenny Brigands Cricket Club with the aim of staging regular matches at the ground. Since that time, first under the auspices of the Royal Navy but later as an independent club, the

Brigands have organised matches and managed the ground. In 1992, the Brigands were assigned the lease by the Royal Navy.

In 1996 the Broadhalfpenny Down Association (BHDA) was set up to secure the future of the ground and, in particular, to encourage young cricketers to play there. Since 1999, Hampshire County matches in age groups ranging from Under 11 to Under 16 have been held at the ground. The association has made a major drive to encourage young people from inner cities, especially from deprived areas, to visit Broadhalfpenny and play cricket. Since 2003 BHDA has hosted matches between Under 13 elevens from inner city community cricket clubs, with all the players coming from ethnic minorities. The Hampshire Primary Special Schools Kwik-cricket Festival has been staged at the ground as the culmination of a county-sponsored cricket teaching programme. BDHA has also expanded the number of matches it sponsors between local teams of young people. In 2004, the association hosted a match between the Hackney Community College Cricket Academy and its own BHDA Invitation XI of young local cricketers. The fixture was repeated in 2005 and has now become a regular. In 2005 more than 60 matches were played on Broadhalfpenny Down, including 20 or more for young cricketers. A synthetic wicket and net were built in 2005 with grants from the Lord Taverners, the Cricket Society Trust, the Michael May Young Cricketers Trust and Hampshire Playing Fields to increase facilities at the ground, especially for young cricketers.

In 1998 BHDA launched an appeal to enable it to build a new pavilion and provide electricity and water to the ground. More than 400 individuals and organisations from all over the world responded, stressing the enormous affection in which the ground is held. On my most recent visit, I met Peter Tuke, the association's chairman, who showed me round the new pavilion with its impressive facilities. The patrons of the association include Dr Ali Bacher, John Barclay, Richie Benaud, Ted Dexter, David Gower, Rachel Heyhoe Flint, Christopher Martin-Jenkins, Lord Maclaurin, Sir John Major, Mark Nicholas and Sir Gary Sobers. The BDHA produces information for visitors on the history of the ground and arranges presentations during lunch and tea intervals during matches. Contact details can be found in the bibliography section at the back of the book.

The Bat and Ball pub survives and thrives, though it has had a turbulent time in recent years. In his splendid memoir Hambledon (revised edition 1994), John Goldsmith has a photograph of the pub in 1951 that shows it was owned at the time by Henty & Constable, a brewery based in Chichester, that was taken over and closed by the giant London company Watney Mann in 1955. The pub then became part of the tied estate of the Guildford brewer Friary Meux, which in turn became part of the national combine, Allied Breweries. The pub probably passed from Watneys to Allied in the late 1970s when Roy Hattersley, Secretary of State for Consumer Protection in Harold Wilson's Labour government, ordered national brewers with a high concentration of pubs in any given area to swap them in order to increase choice for drinkers.

It was under Allied Breweries that the Bat and Ball almost ceased to be a shrine to English cricket. In the early 1990s, in a fit of cultural vandalism, Allied turned the ancient inn into a modern eaterie called Natterjacks, a breed of toad. It was painted lime green and customers were not allowed to sit at the bar and enjoy a drink. All the cricketing memorabilia and artefacts were thrown out. They included ancient scorecards, including one that recorded the match in 1777 when Hambledon beat All England by an innings and 168 runs, old bats and a wealth of fascinating prints and photographs that trace the development of the game in the late eighteenth century. Fortunately, this important collection was saved by local supporters.

Natterjacks was not a success and failed to attract Mr Toad and others more interested in food than good beer and cricket. In 1996, George Gale, the Horndean family-owned brewer, bought the pub and spent the best part of two years restoring it to its old glory as the Bat and Ball and reinstalling all the old artefacts. Today you can still eat well in the spacious restaurant but you can also sit at the bar and sup Gale's beers if you prefer, or visit the Nyren Room and inspect bats, balls and records that trace the history of the game from the time of Hambledon.

In 2005, the London brewer Fuller's of Chiswick bought Gale's. Once again there were concerns for the future of the pub, but Fuller's stressed that it had no plans to make any changes. Gale's beers are still available but they are now brewed at Chiswick. Talks that I have had with representatives of the company indicate that they appreciate the importance of the Bat and Ball and the international love and respect that it enjoys. It is also not lost on Fuller's that Allied Breweries of Natterjacks infamy has gone out of business

## Further Reading

*The Official ECB Guide to Cricket Grounds,*
William A Powell (Sutton, 2003)

*Start of Play, David Underdown*
(Allen Lane The Penguin Press, 2000)

*A Social History of English Cricket,*
Derek Birley (Aurum Press, 2000/2003)

*Hambledon,* John Goldsmith
(Phillimore, 1994)

*Lord's,* Geoffrey Moorhouse
(Hodder & Stoughton, 1983)

*Cricket Facts and Feats,*
Bill Frindall (Guinness, 1993)

*Wisden Book of Cricket Records,*
Bill Frindall (Queen Anne Press, 1981)

*John Arlott's 100 Greatest Batsmen,*
John Arlott (Macdonald /Queen Anne Press,
1989)

*Arlott on Cricket,* edited by David Rayvern
Allen (Collins, 1984)

*Fred,* John Arlott, (Eyre & Spottiswoode 1971)

*Cricket – a Way of Life,*
Christopher Martin-Jenkins (Century, 1984)

*Books that are out of print may neverthe-
less be available from specialist sources
via amazon.co.uk*

## Thanks

During the course of my visits to the First Class grounds I have met some of the most charming and helpful people it has been my pleasure to come across, people with a deep and abiding love of cricket. I began, naturally, at Lord's, where MCC Curator Adam Chadwick and his colleagues gave me the run of their magnificent library and opened many doors at county clubs. My trips began on a wet day in February, 2006, at Leicester, where Sylvia Michael not only showed me round the pavilion but had prepared a 10-page document detailing the history of the club. On another wet day at Trent Bridge, David Wynne-Thomas bubbled with enthusiasm and impressed me not only with his knowledge of the game but his accurate assessment of the number of minutes it would take me to reach the first pub on my list. Trevor Jones at Surrey was a mine of information and produced a print of the Horns pub where the club was founded; how I envy him in his office high above the pavilion with a magnificent view of the Oval. David Robertson at Canterbury took an enormous amount of time in taking me round the pavilion and other areas where the history and artefacts of Kent are stored. Maria Carney at Worcester cheerfully put up with me three times rearranging my visit to New Road. Mike Simpson dodged a downpour, dressed in a raincoat and shorts, to take on a tour of the Bristol ground. I managed to miss John Bridgeman at Edgbaston but thank for him arranging my visit to his splendid museum. Andrew Hignell agreed to see me at Cardiff at short notice, gave generously of his time, joined me for a beer and helped me find the necessary pubs in the city. Rob Boddie at Hove and Neil Jenkinson at the Rose Bowl saw me on days when vital games were being played but still gave generously of their time. In Edinburgh Gordon Tolland, slightly bemused that a Sassenach should want to visit the delightful ground at Raeburn Place, was nevertheless a good host. I ended at Headingley, with the season over and damp underfoot, where David Hall kindly interrupted the other demands on his time in the close season to take me round a ground that has been so brilliantly improved that I scarcely recognised it. Special mention must go to Keith Hayhurst at Lancashire, who sorted out a misunderstanding with my hosts, the brewery that works in association with Andrew Flintoff, which left me in Manchester on the wrong day and without a hotel. Keith drove me to alternative accommodation, picked me up the following morning and returned with me to Old Trafford for a memorable visit to the ground and museum. Sadly, I never got to meet Freddie.

At Hambledon, Pete Tuke, chairman of the Broadhalfpenny Down Association, graciously gave of his time and showed me round the fine new pavilion. Georgina Wald, public relations manager of Fuller's Brewery, and Derek Beaves, formerly of Gale's and now also of Fuller's, were generous hosts at the Bat & Ball.

I am indebted to Joanna Copestick and Debbie Williams at CAMRA Books for their enthusiasm for the project and to Debbie in particular for sorting and improving my pub photos. They both know a little more about cricket than when we started.

Finally, my thanks as always to my wife Diana and sons Adam and Matthew for allowing me to be away from home for even longer stretches than usual. They are still attempting to come to terms with the notion that visiting cricket grounds and pubs constitutes 'work'.

The publishers would also like to thank Peter Yates at the Somerset Cricket Museum for the photograph on page 107 and John Humphreys of Edwards Harvey for arranging photography of the Cricketers Pub sign on the back jacket.

# Picture credits

Front Jacket: Cephas/Mick Rock; centre Corbis/Paul A Souders; right Superstock/Roger Allyn Lee.
Back Jacket: Shepherd Neame

1 CAMRA; 2 Patrick Eagar; 4 Empics/S & G/Alpha; 7 Mick Slaughter; 8-11 courtesy of Gales Brewery; 12-13 Bridgeman Art Library/© Marylebone Cricket Club, London, UK; 16, 19 Roger Protz; 20-23 Patrick Eagar; 24 above & below Empics/S & G/Alpha; 25 Empics/Don Morley; 26 Roger Protz; 27-29 Patrick Eagar; 30 Empics/Rob Griffith/AP; 31-32 Roger Protz; 34-35 Patrick Eagar; 36 above left Empics/PA Photos; 36 centre left Empics/Nick Potts/PA Photos; 36 below left & right Empics/Neal Simpson; 37-39 Roger Protz; 40-41 Patrick Eagar; 42 above Patrick Eagar; 42 below left Empics/Neal Simpson; 42 below centre Empics/Mike Egerton; 42 below right Empics/Owen Humphreys/PA Photos; 43-45 Roger Protz; 46-47 Patrick Eagar; 48 above Empics/PA Photos; 48 below Empics/Tony Marshall; 49-50 Roger Protz; 51 left Roger Protz; 51 right CAMRA/Tony Jerome; 53 Empics/Sean Dempsey; 54-55 Patrick Eagar; 56 Empics/S & G/Alpha; 57 above Empics/S & G/Alpha; 57 centre Empics/Barratts/Alpha; 57 below Empics/S & G/Alpha; 58-59 Roger Protz; 60-61 Patrick Eagar; 62 above Empics/S &G/Alpha; 62 below Empics/PA Photos; 63 above Empics/S &G/Alpha; 63 below Empics/PA Photos; 64 Roger Protz; 65 above Roger Protz; 65 below Patrick Eagar; 66-67 Patrick Eagar; 68 Empics /Barratts/Alpha; 69 above left Empics/Gareth Copley/PA Photos; 69 above right Empics/S & G/Alpha; 69 below Patrick Eagar; 70 Roger Protz; 71 Patrick Eagar; 72-73 Patrick Eagar; 74 left & right Empics/S & G/Alpha; 75 Empics/Tony Marshall; 76-77 Roger Protz; 78-79 Patrick Eagar; 80 above Empics; 80 below Empics/S & G/Alpha; 81 Empics/S & G/Alpha; 82 above Empics/Sean Dempsey; 82 below Patrick Eagar; 83-84 Roger Protz; 86-88 Patrick Eagar; 89 above Empics/Tony Marshall; 89 below Empics; 90-91 Roger Protz; 92-93 Patrick Eagar; 94 Empics/P A Photos; 95 above left Empics/Tony Marshall; 95 above centre Empics/Barratts/Alpha; 95 above right & below Empics/S & G/Alpha; 96-97 Roger Protz; 98-99 Patrick Eagar; 100 above & below Empics/P A Photos; 101 above Empics/Matthew Ashton; 101 below Empics/David Worthy; 102-103 Roger Protz; 104-105 Patrick Eagar; 106 above & below Empics/S & G/Alpha; 107 above Empics/S & G/Alpha; 107 below © Somerset Cricket Museum; 108-109 Roger Protz; 110-111 Patrick Eagar; 112 above © Surrey CCC; 112 below left & below right Empics/Barratts/Alpha; 113 above, below left & right Empics/S & G/Alpha; 114-115 Patrick Eagar; 115 right Empics/David Davies; 116 Roger Protz; 118-119 Patrick Eagar; 120 above, below left & right Empics; 121 above Gettyimages/Hulton Archive/George C Beresford; 121 below Empics/Lindsey Parnaby/P A Photos; 122 above left Empics/P A Photos; 122 below Empics/Gareth Fuller/P A Photos; 124-127 Patrick Eagar; 128 left Empics/Barratts/Alpha; 128 centre Empics; 128 right Empics/Barry Batchelor/P A Photos; 129 above & below Patrick Eagar; 130-131 Roger Protz; 132-133 Patrick Eagar; 134 Empics/S & G/Alpha; 135 above left Empics/S & G/Alpha; 135 above centre Empics/P A Photos; 135 above right Empics/S & G/Alpha; 135 below Empics/Batty Batchelor/P A Photos; 136 left Patrick Eagar; 136 right Roger Protz; 137 Roger Protz; 138-139 Patrick Eagar; 140 above Empics/P A Photos; 140 below Empics/S & G/Alpha; 141-143 Patrick Eagar; 144-145 Roger Protz; 146-147 Empics/Ben Curtis/P A Photos; 148 above Empics/S & G/Alpha; 148 below Empics/Ben Curtis/P A Photos; 149 Empics/P A Photos; 150 above left Empics/David Cheskin/P A Photos; 150 below Empics/Tony Marshall; 150 above right Roger Protz; 151 Roger Protz; 152 © Caledonian Brewery; 153 CAMRA.

Whilst every effort has been made to trace the copyright holders, we apologise in advance for any unintentional omission and would be pleased to insert the appropriate acknowledgement in any subsequent edition.

**Contact details for the Broadhalfpenny Down Association:**

BHDA Secretariat, Millstream International
Harting, Petersfield, Hampshire, GU31 5NS

www.broadhalfpennydown.com
**Email:** BHDA@aol.com

# BOOKS FOR BEER LOVERS

CAMRA Books, the publishing arm of the Campaign for Real Ale, is the leading publisher of books on beer and pubs. Key titles include:

## Good Beer Guide
Editor: **ROGER PROTZ**

The Good Beer Guide is the only guide you will need to find the right pint, in the right place, every time. It's the original and the best independent guide to around 4,500 pubs throughout the UK; in 2002 it was named as one of the Guardian newspapers books of the year and the Sun newspaper rated the 2004 edition in the top 20 books of all time! Now in its 35th year, this annual publication is a comprehensive and informative guide to the best real ale pubs in the UK, researched and written exclusively by CAMRA members and fully updated every year.

£14.99   ISBN 13: 978 1 85249 224 3

## Big Book of Beer
**ADRIAN TIERNEY-JONES**

Everything you could ever want to know about the world's favourite drink; this beautifully illustrated book is an eye-opener to the world of beer articulated by well-known beer experts and those who brew it. A perfect gift for the 'real beer' connoisseur.

£14.99   ISBN 13: 978 1 85249 212 0

## 300 Beers To Try Before You Die
**ROGER PROTZ**

300 beers from around the world, handpicked by award-winning journalist, author and broadcaster Roger Protz to try before you die! A comprehensive portfolio of top beers from the smallest microbreweries in the United States to family-run British breweries and the world's largest brands. This book is indispensable for both beer novices and aficionados.

£12.99   ISBN 13: 978 1 85249 213 7

## Good Pub Food
**SUSAN NOWAK & JILL ADAM**

This fully revised sixth edition of Good Pub Food singles out over 600 real ale pubs in England, Wales, Scotland and Northern Ireland, which also specialise in fine cuisine. All are highlighted on easy to use maps and have a full description of their location, ales, menus, prices, vegetarian selections and facilities. Both Susan Nowak and Jill Adam have been involved in editing and compiling CAMRA guides for over 20 years.

£14.99   ISBN 13: 978 1 85249 214 4

## CAMRA's London Pub Walks
**BOB STEEL**

CAMRA's London Pub Walks enables you to explore the entire city while never being far away from a decent pint. A practical pocket-sized guide, it includes 30 walks around more than 180 pubs serving fine real ale, from the heart of the City and the bustling West End to majestic riverside routes and the leafy common of Wimbledon. The perfect companion for a day out discovering real London.

£8.99 ISBN 13: 978 1 85249 216 8

## Beer, Bed & Breakfast
**SUSAN NOWAK AND JILL ADAM**

A unique and comprehensive guide to more than 500 of the UK's real ale pubs that also offer great accommodation, from tiny inns with a couple of rooms upstairs to luxury gastro-pubs with country-house style bedrooms. All entries include contact details, type and extent of accommodation, beers served, meal types and times, and an easy-to-understand price guide to help plan your budget. This year, why not stay somewhere with a comfortable bed, a decent breakfast and a well-kept pint of beer, providing a home from home wherever you are in the country.

£14.99   ISBN 13: 978 1 85249 230 4

## Stedders Guides
**RICHARD STEDMAN**

Also available via CAMRA Books are the Stedders Football and Real Ale Guides. Richard Stedman has created a nationwide team of football and real ale fans to compile informative guides to the top real ale pubs for every football club in the UK, from the Premiership to League Division 2. Available direct from CAMRA, www.camra.org.uk/books or from Stedders Guides: www.footballandreal-guide.co.uk.

Order these and other CAMRA books online at **www.camra.org.uk/books**, ask at your local bookstore, or contact: CAMRA, 230 Hatfield Road, St Albans, AL1 4LW. Telephone 01727 867201

# Do you feel passionately about your pint?
## Then why not join CAMRA

Just fill in the application form (or a photocopy of it) and the Direct Debit form on the next page to receive three months' membership FREE!

If you wish to join but do not want to pay by Direct Debit, please fill in the application form below and send a cheque, payable to CAMRA, to
**CAMRA, 230 Hatfield Road, St Albans, Hertfordshire, AL1 4LW.**

Please tick appropriate box

|  | Direct Debit | Non Direct Debit |
|---|---|---|
| Single Membership (UK & EU) | £20 ❏ | £22 ❏ |
| For under-26 Membership | £11 ❏ | £13 ❏ |
| For 60 and over Membership | £11 ❏ | £13 ❏ |

For partners' joint membership add £5 (Partner must live at the same address).
Life membership information is available on request.

If you join by Direct Debit you will receive three months' membership extra, free!

Title_____ Surname_____

Forename(s)_____

Address_____

_____ Postcode_____

Date of Birth_____ Email address_____

Signature_____

Partner's details (for Joint Membership)

Title_____ Surname_____

Forename(s)_____

Date of Birth_____ Email address_____

Please tick here c if you would like to receive occasional emails from CAMRA (at no point will your details be released to a third party).

Find out more about CAMRA at **www.camra.org.uk**          Telephone 01727 867201

# It takes all sorts to Campaign for Real Ale

CAMRA, the Campaign for Real Ale, is an independent not-for-profit, volunteer-led consumer group. We actively campaign for full pints and more flexible licensing hours, as well as protecting the 'local' pub and lobbying government to champion pub-goers' rights.

CAMRA has more than 80,000 members from all ages and backgrounds, brought together
by a common belief in the issues that CAMRA deals with and their love of good quality British beer.
For just £20 a year, that's less than a pint a month, you can join CAMRA and enjoy the following benefits:

A monthly colour newspaper informing you about beer and pub news and detailing events and beer festivals around the country.
Free or reduced entry to over 140 national, regional and local beer festivals.
Money off many of our publications including the *Good Beer Guide* and the *Good Bottled Beer Guide*.

Access to a members-only section of our national website,
www.camra.org.uk, which gives up-to-the-minute news stories and includes
a special offer section with regular features saving money on beer and trips away.

The opportunity to campaign to save pubs under threat of closure, for pubs to be open when people want to drink
and a reduction in beer duty that will help Britain's brewing industry survive.

Log onto **www.camra.org.uk** for **CAMRA** membership information.

**CAMPAIGN
FOR
REAL ALE**

---

**CAMPAIGN
FOR
REAL ALE**

## Instruction to your Bank or Building Society to pay by Direct Debit

**DIRECT Debit**

Please fill in the form and send to: Campaign for Real Ale Ltd. 230 Hatfield Road, St. Albans, Herts. AL1 4LW

**Name and full postal address of your Bank or Building Society**

To The Manager                          Bank or Building Society

Address

Postcode

**Name (s) of Account Holder (s)**

**Bank or Building Society account number**

**Branch Sort Code**

**Reference Number**

Banks and Building Societies may not accept Direct Debit Instructions for some types of account

**Originator's Identification Number**

| 9 | 2 | 6 | 1 | 2 | 9 |
|---|---|---|---|---|---|

FOR CAMRA OFFICIAL USE ONLY
This is not part of the instruction to your Bank or Building Society

Membership Number

Name

Postcode

**Instruction to your Bank or Building Society**
Please pay CAMRA Direct Debits from the account detailed on this Instruction subject to the safeguards assured by the Direct Debit Guarantee. I understand that this instruction may remain with CAMRA and, if so, will be passed electronically to my Bank/Building Society

Signature(s)

Date

*detached and retained this section*

**DIRECT Debit**

This Guarantee should be detached and retained by the payer.

## The Direct Debit Guarantee

- This Guarantee is offered by all Banks and Building Societies that take part in the Direct Debit Scheme. The efficiency and security of the Scheme is monitored and protected by your own Bank or Building Society.

- If the amounts to be paid or the payment dates change CAMRA will notify you 7 working days in advance of your account being debited or as otherwise agreed.

- If an error is made by CAMRA or your Bank or Building Society, you are guaranteed a full and immediate refund from your branch of the amount paid.

- You can cancel a Direct Debit at any time by writing to your Bank or Building Society. Please also send a copy of your letter to us.